Steam
A Guide
Preservation Railways

CADOGAN

Cadogan Guides
West End House
11 Hills Place
London W1R 1AH
guides@cadogan.demon.co.uk

The Globe Pequot Press
6 Business Park Road, PO Box 833, Old Saybrook,
Connecticut 06475-0833

Copyright © Cadogan Guides, an imprint of Morris Publications Ltd
1999

Conceived and produced for Cadogan Guides by
The Jacket Front Ltd
postmaster@bookprodservices.demon.co.uk
Designed by Ann Burnham
Cover design by Fielding Rowinski

Written by: Joseph Fullman & G.P. Foreman
Additional contributions and research: Joanne Taborn

ISBN 1-86011-700-7

Colour reproduction by
The Setting Studio, Newcastle upon Tyne
Printed in China by
Leo Paper Products Ltd

Photo Credits
The publishers would like to thank all those railway societies and
organisations who supplied photographs free of charge for this book.
Photographs listed below have detailed copyright: Bideford Railway
Museum © Rob Dark; ©Darlington Railway Centre; North Norfolk Railway
© Steve Allen; Glasgow Museum of Transport © Glasgow Museums;
Strathspey Railway © K. Pirt; Bala Lake, Snowdon Mountain Railway, Teifi
Valley Railway and Welshpool & Llanfair Light Railway © Peter Johnson;
Welsh High Railway © DW Allan

Contents

This 36-acre open-air museum on the site of the former Amberley Chalk Pits holds one of the most extensive collections of narrow gauge rolling stock in the country—thirty locomotives and over forty varieties of wagon and coach. There are also two sections of track. The first is an industrial demonstration line, while the second carries passengers nearly half a mile in all too authentic (unsprung!) quarrymen's coaches. Elsewhere you can see demonstrations of traditional local crafts such as pottery and cobbling in recreated workshops.

AMERTON

In 1987 a group of volunteers came together to rescue and restore 'Isabel', a hundred-year-old steam locomotive. They also decided to build her a new home—the 2ft gauge Amerton Railway. Work has continued ever since and in 1999 a new extension will take the line to around a mile in length. Several other engines have joined 'Isabel' at Amerton, including an 0-4-0 'Dreadnought', built in 1939, a re-gauged 2'6" Ruston and Hornsby diesel and two Simplex locomotives. The line also boasts some beautifully restored rolling stock and a rebuilt 1880s wooden Great Northern platform building.

AUDLEY END

HOW TO FIND US:
By car: Audley End House, just off B1383
Car parking: Free
By rail: Audley End
TEL: 01799 541 354
LENGTH OF LINE: 1.5-mile round trip
OPENING TIMES: Every w/end and bank holiday Mar–Oct; daily during school summer holidays
FACILITIES: Afternoon teas in LT Bus
DISABLED: No wheelchair access to trains, but good access elsewhere

Set in grounds landscaped by Capability Brown and overlooked by Audley End House, a grand Jacobean mansion, this is one of the country's most picturesque railways. Three steam engines and two diesels make the 1.5-mile round trip through shady woodlands across the River Cam and back, turning at an enchantingly laid out garden loop. In summer, concerts are held in the mansion grounds and teas served in a converted 1950s Routemaster.

HOW TO FIND US:
Follow the brown tourist signs from the A444, A447 and B585 roads
Car Parking: Large free car park at Shackerstone; narrowboats can visit and moor by Ashby Canal bridge
ADDRESS:
Shackerstone Station, Shackerstone, Leics, CV13 6NW
TEL: 01827 880 754
LENGTH OF LINE: 4.5 miles
OPENING TIMES: Steam services operate on w/ends and bank holidays between mid-Mar and Nov
FACILITIES: Tea room, buffet on most trains, souvenir shop

BATTLEFIELD

The battle was Bosworth Field, where the bloody Wars of the Roses were settled, and the last king of England to die in battle was slain. You can travel here from Shackerstone, perhaps aboard the special 'Tudor Rose' dining car, to visit the site and the Battlefield Visitor Centre which tells the story of that momentous day in 1485. Shackerstone Station itself, the headquarters of the line, dates from 1873—it celebrated its 125th anniversary in 1998—and houses a fascinating collection of local railway history. Above the Engine Shed is a viewing area overlooking the lines, signal box and Leicestershire countryside.

BEAMISH MUSEUM

HOW TO FIND US:
By car: Follow the signs from the A1 (M) Jct 63
Car parking: Free
By rail: Sunderland and Durham City for buses to Beamish
By bus: Nos 775 and 778 from Sunderland, 720 from Durham,
ADDRESS: Beamish, County Durham
TEL: 01207 231 811
WEBSITE: www. merlins.demon.co.uk/ beamish
OPENING TIMES:
10–5 Apr–Nov;
10–4 Nov–Mar
FACILITIES: Pub, souvenir shops
DISABLED:
Limited wheelchair access

This vast 300-acre open air museum aims to recreate life in 19th-century Northern England. Accompanying the Town, Colliery Village and Home Farm is a Victorian Railway Station, complete with goods yard, signal box, coal cells, locomotives and rolling stock. Due to open in the summer of 1999 is the Pockerley Waggonway, where visitors will be able to relive the very first days of steam travel by riding on carriages pulled by a unique replica of Stephenson's 'Locomotion No 1'. The work of Stephenson and his contemporaries is further explored in an exhibition in The Great Engine Shed, the centrepiece of which will be a splendid 1822 locomotive, reputed to be the third oldest in the world.

HOW TO FIND US:
By car: From Exeter, follow signs along the A3052 to Beer
Car parking: Free car and coach parking
By rail/bus: Buses run from Axminster, call 01392 382 800
ADDRESS: Beer Heights Light Railway, Pecorama, Beer, Seaton, Devon EX12 3NA
TEL: 01297 21542
WEBSITE:
www.mmcltd.co.uk/ peco/
LENGTH OF LINE:
1-mile
OPENING TIMES:
Mon-Sat Apr-Sept; Sun May–Sept; daily during Oct half term
FACILITIES: Licensed Restaurant, refreshments
DISABLED: Wheelchair access

BEER HEIGHTS

Set in the Pecorama Pleasure Gardens, this miniature steam- and diesel-driven railway takes you on a fantastic trip over bridges, past gardens and through tunnels to Deepwater Lake. A new zig-zag section leads down an incline to the disused Beer Mine itself (unfortunately, despite the name, this was a source of chalk rather than ale). The gardens boast many other attractions including an indoor display of model railways, an aviary, an assault course, a wooden maze and crazy golf. In Beer itself, there are some delightful shingle beaches where, in summer, you can hire row boats.

BIDEFORD RAILWAY MUSEUM

HOW TO FIND US:
By car: Follow the A39. The Museum is at the East end of the old Bideford Bridge
Car parking: Free
By rail: Bideford
By bus: Buses between Barnstaple and Bideford stop outside the station
ADDRESS: Bideford Station, Railway Terrace, Bideford, Devon EX39 4BB
TEL: 01237 423 585
OPENING TIMES: Throughout the year, Sun 2–5, Easter–Oct Tues & bank holidays
FACILITIES: Refreshments, book shop, souvenir shop
DISABLED: No wheelchair access

This museum is housed in an old Barnstaple–Torrington line station. Its principal exhibit is an 1870s signal box, built to control the crossing gates and passing loop at Instow station—visitors can now 'pull off' a signal in the carefully restored interior. Various railway vehicles, including a BR Mk 1 carriage, a brake van, a goods van and an SR PMV parcels van are displayed on a short length of track; there are plans to give rides in the brake van in the near future. More entertainment can be found at Bideford's nearby 'Big Sheep' sheep centre where regular sheep steeplechases (or sheeplechases) are run.

BLUEBELL LINE

HOW TO FIND US:
By car: Sheffield Park is on the A275
Car parking: At Sheffield Park and Horsted Keynes
By rail/bus: From East Grinstead I
ADDRESS: Uckfield, E.Sussex TN22 3QL
TEL: 01825 723 777
TALKING TIMETABLE: 01825 722 370
WEBSITE: www.visitweb.com/bluebell
LENGTH OF LINE: 9 miles
OPENING TIMES: W/ends through the year; daily Easter–Sept and school holidays
FACILITIES: Café, real ale bar, gift shop, all at Sheffield Park
DISABLED: Wheelchair access and adapted toilets

The Bluebell, perhaps the country's most famous railway, winds its way through over a century of railway tradition. The headquarters at Sheffield Park is home to the region's largest locomotive collection, as well as a museum of railway memorabilia and a reconstructed signal box, while at Horsted Keynes, possibly the finest preserved station in the country, there is an award-winning carriage and wagon display. Every last detail has been meticulously researched, from the elegant fittings in the sumptuous Pullman dining cars to the period advertisements that adorn the station walls. In spring the trains run through the fields of bluebells which give the line its name.

HOW TO FIND US:
By car: Station is on the B3268
Car parking: Only at Bodmin General
By rail: Bodmin Parkway
By bus: Call 01208 798 898
ADDRESS: Bodmin General Station, Bodmin, Cornwall PL31 1AQ
TEL: 01208 73666
LENGTH OF LINE: 6.5 miles
OPENING TIMES: Daily Apr–Oct
FACILITIES: Buffet and souvenir shop
DISABLED: Limited access

Two lines run from the railway's headquarters at Bodmin General, a restored Great Western Railway station, both affording ample opportunity for picnics, walks and exploration of the Cornish countryside. A newly laid stretch of track leads to Boscarne Junction, the starting point for the 'Camel Trail'—a popular foot and cycle path—while at Colesloggett Halt, on the line to Bodmin Parkway, a footpath leads to the nature trails and cycle tracks of Cardinham Woods. At Bodmin Parkway itself, you can take a scenic walk along to Lanhydrock, a National Trust property.

BOWES

HOW TO FIND US:
By car: Springwell is near Gateshead, just off the B1288
Car parking: Free
By rail: Gateshead
By bus: 184 & 189 from Washington and 187 & 188 from Gateshead
ADDRESS: Bowes Railway, Springwell Village, Gateshead NE9 7QJ
TEL: 01914 161 847
WEBSITE: www.users.pipemedia.net/bowes
LENGTH OF LINE: 1.25 miles
OPENING TIMES: Bank holidays, and the 2nd/4th Sun of each month from Easter–Sept
FACILITIES: Souvenir shop, café
DISABLED: Wheelchair access

Developed to carry coal from the mines of north west Durham to the River Tyne at Jarrow, the Bowes Railway affords a fascinating insight into the area's great industrial heritage. Steam locomotives pull traditional colliery break vans from the museum centre to Blackham's Hill where you can view two working inclines. Designed by George Stephenson in 1826, these are the only preserved standard gauge rope-hauled inclines in the world. A superb collection of colliery wagons is complemented by some magnificent mid-Victorian stone buildings, including a chain-makers, blacksmiths, wagon and tub shops.

BRESSINGHAM STEAM MUSEUM

9

HOW TO FIND US:
By Car: Just off the A1066, 2 miles west of Diss
Car parking: Free
By rail: Diss
ADDRESS: Diss, Norfolk IP22 2AB
TEL: 01379 687 386, 24-hour Infoline: 01379 687 382
OPENING TIMES: Daily Apr–Oct; special events in Dec
FACILITIES: Café, souvenir shop, gardens and plant centre
DISABLED: Wheelchair access; limited number of wheelchairs—adapted toilets

Bressingham offers an unparalleled array of steam attractions, all set in six acres of enchanting gardens. There are no fewer than three different narrow gauge lines—the Nursery Railway, which passes the nearby lake and woodland and gives views of the splendid Roydon church; the Waveney Valley Railway, which runs over watermeadows and through rhododendron banks; and the Garden Railway, home to the 'Alan Bloom', built from scratch by the Bressingham team. The extensive collection of standard gauge locomotives is complemented by traction engines, steam wagons, stationary engines and 'The Gallopers', a magnificent Victorian steam carousel.

HOW TO FIND US:
By car: Just off the A41
Car parking: Free at Quainton Road
By rail: Aylesbury
ADDRESS: Quainton Road Station, Quainton, Aylesbury, Bucks HP22 4BY
TEL: 01296 655720
INFOLINE: 01296 655450
LENGTH OF LINE: 2.5 miles
OPENING TIMES: Sun and bank holidays from Easter–Oct; Wed June–Aug
FACILITIES: Gift and book shop, secondhand bookshop, refreshments
DISABLED: Wheelchair access and adapted toilets

BUCKINGHAMSHIRE RAILWAY CENTRE

The beautifully preserved Victorian station at Quainton Road, which today houses the Buckinghamshire Railway Centre, was once a stop on the Metropolitan and Great Central line from Victoria to Verney Junction. It holds a huge collection of locomotives, carriages and wagons as well as railway memorabilia from all over the world. You can take a ride on the exquisitely crafted tiny locomotives that chug around its miniature railway or live out that schoolboy dream and learn to drive a steam engine on one of their special courses. The railway also organises various events throughout the year, including a Miniature Traction Engine Rally, a Fire Fighting Day and an Autumn Steam Spectacular.

BURE VALLEY

10

HOW TO FIND US:
By car: A140
Car parking: Free at Wroxham and Aylsham
By rail: Wroxham
By bus: From Aylsham and Wroxham
TEL: 01263 733 858
WEBSITE: www.grail.co.uk/bvr
LENGTH OF LINE: 9 miles
OPENING TIMES: From Easter–Oct
FACILITIES: Café, picnic area, shop
DISABLED: Wheelchair access

Four steam locomotives operate on this 15″ gauge line, Norfolk's longest narrow gauge railway, transporting up to 250 passengers at a time in luxurious uphol-stered coaches. The journey begins in the old market town of Aylsham, where there are workshops, a small museum and a model railway, and finishes at Wroxham, 'The Capital of the Broads'—combined train and boat excursions are available.

CADEBY LIGHT RAILWAY

HOW TO FIND US:
By car: Cadeby is on the A447, six miles north of Hinckley
Car parking: Available on site
By rail: Hinckley
By bus: No.178 from Hinckley to Nuneaton stops at the railway
ADDRESS: The Old Rectory, Cadeby, Nuneaton, Warks CV13 0AS
TEL: 01455 290 462
OPENING TIMES: Second Sat of every month throughout the year
FACILITIES: Refreshments

The Cadeby Light Railway was founded by the late Reverend Teddy Boston, the original 'Fat Controller' of the Thomas the Tank Engine books, and is one of the smallest full-size passenger railways in the world. It is also home to a number of other attractions including a large model railway, a miniature 5″ gauge passenger-carrying line and a 'Fiery Elias', a Foster agricultural engine. There's also a popular brass-rubbing centre in the nearby 13th-century church of All Saints. The railway hosts various special events throughout the year including a Morris Dance Day in May and a Teddy Bears Picnic in June.

CHASEWATER

Chasewater Railway was built in the 1870s to speed up the transport of coal from the Cannock Chase Coalfield to the hungry Black Country industries—it had previously been transported by canal. Today you can take a ride from Brownhills West, where there is a display of engines and carriages, across a quarter-mile-long causeway to Norton Lakeside. This adjoins the Norton Wildfowl Reserve, home to various species of local wildlife, including 18 kinds of dragonfly

CHINNOR & PRINCES RISBOROUGH

The Chinnor and Princes Risborough Railway Association formed in 1989 to restore part of the disused Watlington branch or 'Icknield Line'. Every weekend visitors are invited to take a ride through four miles of charming countryside from Oxfordshire into Buckinghamshire and back again. The Association owns seven locomotives, the oldest built in 1916, and there are regular visits by 'guest' engines from around the country. Other attractions in the area include Rycote, a 15th-century chapel, which provided the setting for the wedding scene in the recent BBC production of *Jane Eyre*, and Thame, a lovely unspoilt village where medieval timber frame buildings stand next to stately Georgian town houses.

CHOLSEY & WALLINGFORD

HOW TO FIND US:
By car: Cholsey is on the A329
Car parking: Ample parking space
By rail: Cholsey
ADDRESS: Cholsey & Wallingford Railway, St Johns Road, Wallingford, Oxon
TEL: 0118 972 3571
24 hr Infoline 01491 835 067
LENGTH OF LINE: 2.5 miles
OPENING TIMES: W/end and holiday dates from April–Oct
FACILITIES: Café, shop at Wallingford

This restored line, from part of the old Great Western Railway, takes its passengers on a ride through the leafy Oxfordshire country-side. The line was originally opened in 1866, and is one of the oldest surviving G.W.R. lines in the Thames Valley. The museum at Wallingford, one of the oldest chartered towns in the country, holds a collection of local railway miscellanea, including a model of the original station as it would have appeared in around 1930 and an 'N' gauge model railway.

CHURNET VALLEY

HOW TO FIND US:
By car: Cheddleton is on the A570
Car parking: Opposite the station
By rail: Stoke-on-Trent or Blythe Bridge stations
TEL: 01538 360 522
ADDRESS: Cheddleton Station, Cheddleton, Staffordshire Moorlands, ST13 7EE
OPENING TIMES: Steam trains run every Sun and bank holiday from late Mar–early Oct and every Wed in Aug
LENGTH OF LINE: 6.5-mile round trip
FACILITIES: Picnic island, tea rooms and souvenir shop
DISABLED: Wheelchair access to most of the site; train rides by arrangement

In the heart of the Staffordshire moor-lands, the Churnet Valley Railway aims to recreate the atmosphere and ambience of a 1950s steam-operated country line. The line is being gradually restored and reopened to the public. Currently it runs from the hand-some Victorian station at Cheddleton through one of the longest tunnels on Britain's preserved railways to the beautiful 'Hidden Valley' at Consall. Cheddleton's famous flint museum, with its collection of 17th- and 18th-century water-mills, is just a short walk away.

CLEETHORPES COAST LIGHT RAILWAY

HOW TO FIND US:
By car: Lakeside is
on the Cleethorpes
resort road
Car parking: On site
By rail: Cleethorpes
By bus: No.17
ADDRESS:
Cleethorpes Coast
Light Railway Ltd,
Kings Road,
Cleethorpes, Lincs
DN35 0AG
TEL: 01472 604 657
OPENING TIMES:
W/ends all year
round, daily
Good Fri–Sept
FACILITIES: Tea
rooms at Lakeside,
souvenir shop at
Kingsway Station
DISABLED: Wheel-
chair access to
stations

This friendly, family-run steam railway is the only one of its kind left in Lincolnshire. Coasting along from Kingsway to Lakeside, it offers jolly little trips around and through the local scenery; on one side is the holiday fun of Lakeside Park, on the other the varied wildlife and busy shipping lanes of the Humber Estuary. Nearby attractions include Cleethorpe's ancient church and Fuschia Fantasy, a collection of hundreds of varieties of fuschia.

COLNE VALLEY

HOW TO FIND US:
By car: NW of
Braintree on A1017
Car parking: On site
By rail: Braintree
By bus: No. 88/89
ADDRESS: Yeldham
Road, Castle
Hedingham,
Essex CO9 3DZ
TEL: 01787 461 174
WEBSITE: www.
ourworld.
compuserve.com/
homepages/cvhr
LENGTH OF LINE:
1 mile
OPENING TIMES:
11–5, Mar– Dec
(dusk if earlier)
FACILITIES: Buffet,
picnic area, Pullman
restaurant train
DISABLED:
Wheelchair access
to most of the site

A highly successful reconstruction of a typical Essex country branch line, this attractive railway on the banks of the River Colne now carries as many passengers per year as it did in its heyday. Part of its success is due to its promotion of luxury travel. The opulent ambience of the Orient Express is evoked on its Pullman train, featuring beautifully restored Pullman coaches, a bar/reception coach, as well as an exhibition coach and generator van. Passengers also have the chance to become Hercule Poirot for a night on one of the railway's occasional Murder Mystery Evenings.

DARLINGTON MUSEUM

14

HOW TO FIND US:
By car: North of Darlington town centre
Car parking: Free on site
By rail: Darlington North
ADDRESS: North Road Station, Darlington DL3 6ST
TEL: 01325 460 532
OPENING TIMES: 10–5 daily, closed throughout Jan
FACILITIES: Refreshment area, gift and book shop
DISABLED: Wheelchair access, disabled parking facilities

Darlington is one of the great names of railway history. The Stockton and Darlington Railway was opened in 1825 by George Stephenson's 'Locomotion'—the locomotive that pulled the world's first passenger train. Stephenson also surveyed the route and was the company's first engineer. The Locomotion is just one of the exhibits in the centre's remarkable collection of engines, carriages and wagons. There is also a large model railway and, in the Locomotive Works, you can see a new Pacific locomotive being built. Not far away is Skerne Bridge, pictured on the back of the Bank of England five-pound note. Steam train rides over a short length of line are available on special days.

DEAN FOREST

HOW TO FIND US:
By car: Lydney is on the B4234
Car parking: Free car park at Norchard
By rail: Lydney Junction
ADDRESS: Dean Forest Railway Co. Ltd, Forest Road, Lydney, Glos GL15 4ET
TEL: 01594 845840
INFORMATION LINE: 01594 843423
LENGTH OF LINE: 2 miles
OPENING TIMES: Sun April–Sept, Wed in June and July, Thurs and Sat in Aug
FACILITIES: Shop at Norchard, picnic area, refreshments available
DISABLED: Wheelchair access to both museum and trains

The Dean Forest Railway, or 'Friendly Forest Line' is a charming two-mile excursion through one of Britain's best-loved forests, a hilly woodland of ponds, streams and stepping stones. This is no isolated beauty spot, however. For centuries many people's livelihoods have depended on their ability to work the forest. You can find out more about the living history of the area at the Dean Heritage Centre where there is a recreated forester's cottage, a water wheel and a beam engine. The railway itself runs between the mainline Lydney Junction and Norchard Railway Centre, where there is a small railway museum.

DERBY INDUSTRIAL MUSEUM

HOW TO FIND US:
By car: City centre
Car parking: Local parking only
By rail: Derby
ADDRESS: Derby Industrial Museum, Full Street, Derby, DE1 3AR
TEL: 01332 255 308
OPENING TIMES: Mon 11–5, Tue–Sat 10–5, Sun and bank holidays 2–5
FACILITIES: Museum shop, baby-changing facilities
DISABLED: Wheelchair access; parking by prior arrangement

Housed in a former silk mill, this museum has collected a vast range of exhibits designed to illustrate Derby's industrial heritage. The entire history of the technical age is represented; from George Fletcher's 1850 beam engine to the Rolls Royce RB211 Turbofan aeroplane engine—the museum has the finest collection of Rolls Royce aero engines in the world. The story of the Midland railway industry and its effect on Derby is told in the Railway Galleries, where there is a model railway, a replica signal box and, for those interested in the future of railways rather than simply preserving the past, a Railway Research Centre which looks at the possible form and uses of the railways of tomorrow.

DERWENT VALLEY

HOW TO FIND US:
By car: Off the A166 Bridlington road
Car parking: free
By rail: York
By bus: York Station to Stamford Bridge service stops at park
ADDRESS: Derwent Valley Light Railway, Murton Park, Murton Lane, York YO1 3UF
TEL: 01904 489 966
LENGTH OF LINE: 0.5 miles
OPENING TIMES: Park open daily Feb–Oct. The railway runs Sun and bank holidays from Easter–Sept and during Dec for Santa Specials
FACILITIES: Refreshments, souvenir shop
DISABLED: some wheelchair access

The delightful Murton Park, three miles east of York, is home to a Museum of Farming, containing several rare breeds of livestock plus various ancient and rather dangerous looking pieces of farming equipment; an ersatz Dark Age Settlement where you can wander through reconstructed wattle and daub huts; a small maze; various picnic and play areas; and, of course, the Derwent Valley Light Railway. Formerly known as the Blackberry line, this opened in 1993 and trips its way through half a mile of pleasant Yorkshire countryside. The railway has a large collection of locomotives and a restored signal box as well as various items of rolling stock.

DEVON RAILWAY CENTRE

HOW TO FIND US:
By car: 10 minutes from Exeter and just 4 miles from Tiverton on the A396
Car parking: On site
By rail: Exeter
By bus: 55 and 55A
ADDRESS: Devon Railway Centre, Bickleigh, near Tiverton, Devon EX16 8RG
TEL: 01884 855 671
OPENING TIMES: Sun and bank holidays from Easter–Oct; Sun in Nov and Dec; daily during school holidays
FACILITIES: Refreshments and souvenirs
DISABLED: No wheelchair access

The Devon Railway Centre is located in the picturesque village of Bickleigh, next to the famous Bickleigh Bridge. Its centrepiece is a lovingly restored Victorian Great Western station complete with locomotives (including one built in 1931), carriages and wagons. There is also a jaunty little model railway. Bickleigh Castle is a short walk away: a charming fortified medieval manor containing Devon's oldest building—a delightful 11th-century chapel. Inside are exhibitions on the civil war and maritime history. The Centre also makes a pleasant base for exploring the wild open spaces of Exmoor, 10 miles to the north, with its fast streams, wooded valleys, age-old oaks and herds of wild deer.

DIDCOT RAILWAY CENTRE

HOW TO FIND US:
By car: On the A4130
By rail: Didcot Parkway
By bus: Stagecoach and Oxford and Thames Travel
ADDRESS: Great Western Society Ltd, Didcot Railway Station, Didcot, Oxon, OX11 7NJ
TEL: 01235 817 200
LENGTH OF LINE: 1,000 yards
OPENING TIMES: W/ends throughout the year; Apr–Sept and school holidays daily
FACILITIES: Refreshments, picnic area, gift shop
DISABLED: Steps at subway entrance, call in advance for wheelchair assistance

Designed and engineered by Isambard Kingdom Brunel, the Great Western Railway ran from Bristol to London for over a century. Today it is remembered, recreated and celebrated at this living museum in Didcot, the focus of which is the engine shed, housing a collection of over 20 steam locomotives. A reproduction 1839 Firefly is currently being built in the Locomotive Works. There's also a recreation of a typical branch line and country station as well as regular signalling demonstrations and 'Steam' days, including special travelling Post Office days when you can find out how mailbags used to be exchanged at speed.

EAST ANGLIA TRANSPORT MUSEUM

HOW TO FIND US:
By car: Off the A12
Car parking: Car park adjacent
By rail: Oulton
By bus: Nos L11, L12, L18, L19
ADDRESS: Chapel Road, Carlton Colville, Lowestoft, Suffolk NR33 8BL
TEL: 01502 518 459
LENGTH OF LINE: 300 yards
OPENING TIMES: Sun and bank holidays May–Sept; Wed and Sat from June–Sept; every w/day from end of July–1st Sept
FACILITIES: Picnic area, souvenir and gift shop

Home to the East Suffolk Light Railway, a 2ft gauge line which wends its way through some of the three acres of woodland surrounding the museum. The railway began operating in 1973 and is an authentic recreation of a typical mid-century passenger-carrying light railway—many of its features, including the track and signal box, were rescued from discontinued lines elsewhere in the country. The museum itself contains a reconstructed 1930s street scene with working trains, trams and trolley cars.

HOW TO FIND US:
By car: From the A256, take turning for Eythorne and follow signs for EKR
By rail: Shepherdswell
By bus: From Canterbury, Dover, Sandwich and Folkestone. Call 01227 472 082
ADDRESS: Sheperdswell Station, Sheperdswell, Dover, Kent
TEL: 01304 832 042
LENGTH OF LINE: 4-mile round trip
OPENING TIMES: W/ends Easter–end Sept
FACILITIES: Buffet, book and souvenir shop
DISABLED: Limited wheelchair access

EAST KENT

The original East Kent Railway was built early this century to serve the area's collieries. It was one of several lines across the country engineered and run by Colonel H F Stephens in his own distinctive style— *i.e.* cheaply. He used antiquated locomotives and stock, and the lines were characterised by steep inclines and sharp curves. An exhibition at Shepherdswell, the railway's current headquarters, tells the story of the line and this interesting character. The station itself is a recreation of the one which stood here until the 1950s.

EAST LANCASHIRE

HOW TO FIND US:
By car: A58, just off
the M66, Jct 2
Car parking: On site
By rail: Bury
By bus: From
Manchester, Bolton,
Rochdale and
Burnley
ADDRESS: Bolton
Street Station, Bury,
Lancashire, BL9 0EY
TEL: 0161 764 7790
LENGTH OF LINE:
8 miles
OPENING TIMES:
W/ends and bank
holidays Jan–Nov;
Fri in July and Aug;
Santa Specials in
Dec
FACILITIES: Tea
Rooms
Disabled:
Wheelchair access

A wide range of lovingly restored steam and diesel locomotives carry passengers between the five scenic towns on this line. There are plenty of attractions to be found along the way including Irwell Vale's colourful gardens, the Victorian mill at Summerseat, the Heritage Centre at Ramsbottom and the art galleries, museums and dry ski slope at Bury. The railway also organises occasional 'Wine & Dine' trains.

EAST SOMERSET

HOW TO FIND US:
By car: Cranmore is
just off the A361
By rail: Frome
By bus: From
Shepton Mallet
ADDRESS: Cranmore
Railway Station,
Shepton Mallet,
Somerset BA4 4QP
Tel: 01749 880 417
LENGTH OF LINE:
2.75 miles
OPENING TIMES:
Trains run on Sun
Jan–Mar and Nov;
Sat and Sun in April,
May and Oct,
Wed–Sun in June
and Sept; daily
July–Aug
FACILITIES:
Licensed restaurant,
art gallery, video
coach, playground
DISABLED:
Wheelchair access

One of only two remaining all-steam railways in the country, it was founded in 1974 by the wildlife artist and conservationist David Shepherd on the site of the original East Somerset Railway or 'Strawberry Line' which first started operating in 1858. There is a fine replica Victorian Engine Shed where some of the country's most famous locomotives are housed including the 'Black Prince', the 'Green Knight' and an 1877 tank engine. There is also a nature reserve and art gallery where prints of Mr Shepherd's works are displayed. The nearby Cranmore Tower, a 19th-century folly, affords good views of the surrounding countryside.

HOW TO FIND US:
By car: A22 towards
Eastbourne
Car parking: On-site
By rail: Eastbourne
By bus: Call 01323
416 416
Address: EMSR,
Loftbridge Drove,
Eastbourne, East
Sussex BN23 6NS
TEL: 01323 520 229
LENGTH OF LINE:
Nearly 1 mile
OPENING TIMES:
10–5 April–Sept;
w/ends in Oct; daily
during Autumn half
term
FACILITIES: Café,
picnic areas,
souvenir/gift shop
DISABLED: Limited
wheelchair access

Lovingly built and operated by Mike and Rachel Wadey, this miniature steam railway hauls its passengers around the five acres of Southbourne lake, passing through Padgham Tunnel and over Southbourne Crossing on the way. Also on show are a model railway, a garden railway and a locomotive display. For younger visitors there's an adventure playground, nature walk and maze.

HOW TO FIND US:
By car: M27 Jct 5,
take the A335
towards Eastleigh
Car parking: On site
By rail:
Southampton Airport
station
ADDRESS: Lakeside
Country Park, Wide
Lane, Eastleigh,
Hampshire
TEL: 01703 636 612
WEBSITE: www.
steamtrain.co.uk
LENGTH OF LINE:
1.25 miles
OPENING TIMES:
Every Sun
throughout the year
and daily during
school holidays
FACILITIES:
Refreshments,
souvenir shop
DISABLED: No wheel-
chair access onto
carriages, good
access elsewhere

EASTLEIGH LAKESIDE

This 7 25" gauge railway runs from Eastleigh Parkway through some delight-fully leafy countryside to Monks Brook Halt—the journey takes a little over 20 minutes. It has a fascinating collection of locomotives including a 1932 model which makes appearances up and down the country as 'Gordon' in Thomas the Tank Engine events, a 1947 locomotive built for display in a glass case and run for the first time in 1989 and, as a concession to modernity, a miniature replica of the Eurostar Power Car built by a group of students from Southampton University as a project for their degree course.

HOW TO FIND US:
By car: M1 Jct 36, follow brown tourist signs along A6135
Car parking: Free
By rail: Barnsley
ADDRESS: Wath Road, Elsecar, Barnsley S74 8HJ
TEL: 01266 740 203
LENGTH OF LINE: 1 mile
OPENING TIMES: 10–5 daily
FACILITIES: Refreshments
DISABLED: Full wheelchair access and disabled toilets

The centre's full-sized steam railway is just one of a range of exhibits designed to illustrate the industrial history of this area. There is also an interactive science centre; a history centre, where you can try on a variety of Victorian costumes; and over twenty-five craft workshops making everything from candles to dolls' house furniture. The museum's showpiece exhibit is the world-famous Newcomen Beam Engine, built in 1795 to pump water from the local mines. The railway itself runs on Sundays alongside the Dearne and Dove Canals which were once used to convey iron and coal to and from the workshops

HOW TO FIND US:
By car: Just off the A59, near Skipton
Car parking: On site
By rail: Skipton
By bus: From Skipton town centre
ADDRESS: Bolton Abbey Station, Skipton, North Yorks BD23 6AF
TEL: 01756 794 727
TALKING TIMETABLE: 01756 795 189
LENGTH OF LINE: 4.5 miles
OPENING TIMES: Sun through the year, Sat in June and Sept, daily from late July–Aug
FACILITIES: Bolton Abbey Station: Gift shop, refreshment rooms. Embsay: Café, gift and book-shop, picnic area
DISABLED: Wheelchair access

EMBSAY & BOLTON

A trip aboard this jaunty little steam railway is a great way of exploring the craggy limestone landscape that inspired the Romantic visions of Wordsworth and Turner. Embsay Station, built in 1888, is home to an extensive collection of tank engines. From here you can travel on through the North Yorkshire countryside to the reconstructed Bolton Abbey Station, perhaps stopping to picnic at Holywell Halt. Bolton Abbey, home to the rare 'Bee Orchid', is a lovely village and provides a good base for exploring 75 miles of footpaths through some truly dramatic scenery. Other attractions include the 12th-century priory and fortified Barden Tower.

EXMOOR STEAM RAILWAY

HOW TO FIND US:
By car: Bratton
Fleming is just off
the A39
Car parking: Free
By rail: Barnstaple
ADDRESS: Cape of
Good Hope Farm,
Bratton Fleming,
Barnstaple, North
Devon EX22 7JN
TEL: 01598 710711
LENGTH OF LINE:
2 miles
OPENING TIMES:
Sun from late
Mar–Oct; Tue and
Wed in Oct;
Mon–Thurs from
May–Sept; Fri in Aug
FACILITIES: teas,
light lunches, gift
shop, play area
DISABLED: No wheel-
chair access

Its title is something of a misnomer; this friendly, family-run narrow gauge railway is actually about 10 miles west of the great windswept moor. Nonetheless, it has a delightful setting in the sleepy rural village of Bratton Fleming where half-size specially built steam trains wind their way through two miles of lovely Devon countryside. There's also a small display of traction engines. The railway is just a few miles away from Exmoor Zoological Park (also not in Exmoor), home to a variety of rare and endangered animals; and Arlington Court which contains a wonderful collection of Victorian curios.

HOW TO FIND US:
By car: At Blythe
Bridge, off the A50
Car parking: Car
park at Blythe Bridge
By rail: Blythe
Bridge
ADDRESS: Foxfield
Steam Railway,
Blythe Bridge,
Stoke-on-Trent
TEL: 01782 396 210
(weekends), 01270
874 959 (weekdays)
LENGTH OF LINE:
2.5 miles
OPENING TIMES:
Trains operate Sun
and bank holidays
April–Sept
FACILITIES:
Refreshments and
souvenir shop
DISABLED:
Wheelchair access

FOXFIELD

In the heart of the potteries; the ride may not be quite as delicate and refined as a Wedgwood tea service but, in its own way, is just as enjoyable. Built in 1893 to connect a colliery with the national rail system, today the Foxfield Steam Railway provides a genial 2.5 mile ride through some scenic Staffordshire countryside. There's also a standing collection of locomotives and rolling stock. The visitor centres of the Royal Daulton, Spode and Wedgwood factories, where you can see potters crafting the still greatly revered (and greatly expensive) fine china, are all within a few miles' radius.

The GWR or 'Friendly Line' once formed part of the Great Western route from Birmingham to Cheltenham. Since 1983 volunteers have been reconstructing the line, and plan eventually to extend it to Cheltenham Racecourse. The journey through the Cotswolds provides some superb views of the Malvern Hills and far-away Welsh mountains beyond the Vale of Evesham as well as a trip through the 693-yard Greet Tunnel. The prestigious 'City of Truro' and 'Flying Scotsman' locomotives have, in recent years, paid visits to the line.

GREAT CENTRAL

The Great Central Railway, which was once part of a network that ran from Manchester to Marylebone, aims to recreate the experience of main line rail travel during the heyday of steam locomotives. The northern terminus is the wonderfully preserved Loughborough Central Station, built in 1897, which houses a museum of railway artefacts and a large fleet of restored locomotives. From here, the journey takes in restored World War II buildings, brick and steel viaducts, woodland scenery, a marshalling yard and a gas-lit country station before finally finishing up at Leicester North Station.

GREAT COCKROW

A miniature railway which takes itself very seriously, the Great Cockrow offers authentic operation and full signalling with strict block working over nearly two miles of track. Thus it caters for both the serious railway enthusiast and the more casual visitor. There are two routes—the Green takes in the Greywood Tunnel and the 'wild' animals of Jungle Halt, whilst the Red traverses a 45ft viaduct. The twice-daily 'Gladesman', the flagship train, covers both the Red and Green routes in a single journey, as does the occasional 'Burwood Belle'.

HOLLYBUSH

A delightful 7.25″ gauge miniature railway that jogs its way around Cannock's award-winning Holly Bush Garden Centre and its associated nature reserve, home to deer, swans, geese and even wallabies. The carriages are pulled by both diesel and steam locomotives, and there are various examples of scaled replica railway equipment, including some exquisitely rendered miniature signals. The centre itself houses one of the largest collections of fish in the country, with over 240 tanks displaying everything from Guppy to Piranha.

IRONBRIDGE

HOW TO FIND US:
By car: Off M54
Car parking: On site
By bus: Midland Red and Elcocks
ADDRESS:
Ironbridge, Telford, Shropshire TF8 7AW
TEL: 01952 433522
WEBSITE:
www.ironbridge.org.uk/
OPENING TIMES:
Summer 10–6 daily, winter 10–5
FACILITIES: Licensed Victorian pub, sweet shop and tea rooms
DISABLED:
Wheelchair access and adapted toilets

The quiet Shropshire town of Coalbrookdale became, in the late 18th century, the birthplace of the Industrial Revolution. The town, which would soon become the biggest iron-making area in the world, produced the world's first iron rails, boats and trains and, indeed, the first iron bridge; an accomplishment which so impressed the local inhabitants that they renamed the town after it. The fabulous Ironbridge Museum is spread over a 50-acre, six-mile long site at Blists Hill. The principal railway exhibit is a replica of the first ever steam rail locomotive (produced some 26 years before Stephenson's 'Rocket'), designed by Richard Trevithick and built in Ironbridge in 1802.

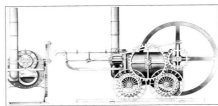

ISLE OF WIGHT

HOW TO FIND US:
By car: Clearly signed on island
Car parking: Free
By rail: Haven Street
By bus: call 01983 562 492
By ferry: Hovercraft (01983 811 000), Red Funnel Ferries (01703 333 042)
ADDRESS: Haven Street, Isle of Wight, PO33 4DS
TEL: 01983 882 204
TALKING TIMETABLE: 01983 884 343
LENGTH OF LINE: 5 miles
OPENING TIMES:
Thurs and Sun late Mar–April and Oct; daily June–Sept
FACILITIES: Licensed café, gift shop, picnic area
DISABLED:
Wheelchair access

The geographic isolation of the Isle of Wight's railway has meant that a greater proportion of its Victorian and Edwardian rolling stock has survived than at most other national lines. At Haven-street Station, the nerve centre of the railway, you can visit the collection of Island Railway artefacts and see locomotives being shunted and worked upon. From here you can travel to Wootton Station, a delightful country terminus complete with old wooden booking office and signal box. The railway plays host to various events throughout the year, including brake van rides, BBQ evenings and a Summer Extravaganza.

KEIGHLEY & WORTH VALLEY

HOW TO FIND US:
By car: NE of Bradford on A650
Car parking: Free
By rail: Leeds
ADDRESS: Haworth, Keighley, West Yorks BD22 8NJ
TEL: 01535 645 214
24-HOUR INFOLINE: 01535 647 317
WEBSITE: www.kwvr.co.uk
LENGTH OF LINE: 4.75 miles
OPENING TIMES: Every w/end and bank holiday; daily mid June–early Sept
FACILITIES: Shops, buffets, picnic areas
DISABLED: Wheelchair access by prior arrangement

Britain's last remaining complete branch line railway runs from Keighley to Oxenhope, along a rich seam of West Yorkshire's rail and cultural heritage. Travel via Ingrow, with its museum and workshops, and Damems, the country's smallest station, to Oakworth where *'The Railway Children'* was filmed. From here, ride on to Haworth, home to another famous family—the Brontës. The line terminates at Oxenhope, where there is a collection of reserve rolling stock.

KENT & EAST SUSSEX

HOW TO FIND US:
By car: A28 between Ashford & Hastings
Car parking: Free parking is available
By rail/bus: Ashford; from here take no. 400 to Tenterden
ADDRESS: Tenterden, Kent TN30 6HE
TEL: 01580 765 155
TALKING TIMETABLE: 01580 762 943
WEBSITE: www.seetb. org.uk/kesr
LENGTH OF LINE: 7 miles
OPENING TIMES: Sun in Mar; w/ends and bank holidays April–Oct; Tues–Thurs in June and Sept; daily in July and Aug;
FACILITIES: Café
DISABLED: Disabled parking, adapted toilets, wheelchair access to carriages

The first line to be built under the Light Railways Act of 1896—and the first full size light railway in the world—the Kent and East Sussex Railway opened in 1900. It has been carefully restored by a team of dedicated volunteers, and now carries passengers through seven scenic miles of Kentish countryside. A 'must-see' is the Colonel Stephens Railway Museum beside Tenterden Town Station, an exhibition detailing the life and work of the enigmatic founder of this and many other great railways. This award-winning museum also houses the 'Gazelle'—the smallest standard gauge steam engine in the world.

KEW BRIDGE STEAM MUSEUM

HOW TO FIND US:
Underground:
Gunnersbury or Kew
Bridge
By rail: Kew Bridge
By bus: Nos 65, 237
267, 391
ADDRESS:
Green Dragon Lane,
Brentford,
Middlesex TW8 0EN
TEL: 0181 568 4757
WEBSITE:
www.cre.canon.co.
uk/~davide/kbsm
LENGTH OF LINE:
100 yards
OPENING TIMES:
11–5 daily; call
FACILITIES:
Café at weekends
DISABLED: Limited
wheelchair access,
large print guide for
the visually impaired

This unique museum focuses on the development of London's water supply from Roman times to the Thames Ring Main. It houses a wonderful collection of Victorian water pumping machinery, including a walk-through Cornish beam engine, and there are peep holes through which you can view the London sewer system. Many Victorian waterworks had their own steam railways and locomotives and examples of these subterranean craft are displayed on a short stretch of line—the prime exhibit is 'Cloister', a Hunslet engine fresh from refurbishment in the Museum workshop.

KIRKLEES

HOW TO FIND US:
By car: Clayton
West Terminus is
just off the A636
Car parking: Free on
site
By rail: Denby Dale.
By bus: 235 from
Huddersfield and
484 from Wakefield
ADDRESS: Kirklees
Light Railway
Company Co. Ltd,
Clayton West, nr
Huddersfield, West
Yorkshire HD8 9XJ
TEL: 01484 865 727
LENGTH OF LINE:
4 miles
OPENING TIMES:
Every W/end
through the year;
every day
Easter–early Sept
FACILITIES: Café and
souvenir shop
DISABLED: Limited
wheelchair access

This recently constructed 15" gauge railway has been laid on the old Lancashire & Yorkshire Clayton branch line which used to feed the main Huddersfield–Sheffield line. From Clayton West, purpose-built half-size steam trains jog through four miles of gently rolling countryside, passing through a 500-yard tunnel on the way. There is a network of country walks in the surrounding area and picnic facilities are provided at both ends. A new visitor centre opened in 1998, where the history of the line and area are explained. There is also an ornamental pond circled by a model railway.

HOW TO FIND US:
By car: Junction 36 off the M6 and follow the signs on the A590 Newby Bridge Road
Car parking: Free
By rail: Windermere
ADDRESS:
Haverthwaite Station, Nr Ulverston, Cumbria LA12 8AL
TEL: 01539 531594
LENGTH OF LINE:
3.5 miles
OPENING TIMES:
Daily during Easter school holidays and May–Oct. Specials in Dec
FACILITIES: Souvenir shop, picnic area, refreshments

Arguably the country's most scenic journey, it begins aboard one of the Lakeside and Haverthwaite's narrow gauge steam trains as it puffs its way past the lakes, rivers and mountains of Cumbria's poet-inspiring countryside. At the terminus at Lakeside there is an opportunity to continue your trip aboard one of the Windermere Lake Cruises elegant 1930s steamers for a tour around England's largest and most beautiful lake. There are a variety of attractions bordering the lake including the Windermere Steamboat Museum, the Lake District National Park Visitor Centre, with its 30 acres of terraced gardens, and the Aquarium of the lakes, home to the largest collection of freshwater fish in England.

HOW TO FIND US:
By car: Off the A30
Car parking: At the nearby Newport Industrial Estate
By rail: Gunnislake
By bus: Sundays by Nos 187 and 188
ADDRESS: The Old Gasworks, St Thomas's Road, Launceston PL15 8DA
TEL: 01566 775 665
LENGTH OF LINE:
2.5 miles
OPENING TIMES:
Tues and Sun Easter–Whitsun; daily Whitsun–end Sept; Tues and Sun in Oct; specials in Dec
FACILITIES: Station buffet, gift and book shop
DISABLED:
Wheelchair access to most areas

LAUNCESTON

The four locomotives maintained and run on this famous narrow gauge railway were built in the 1880s and '90s by the Hunslet Engine Company of Leeds, and worked carrying slate from the mountain quarries of North Wales. Nowadays they carry passengers from the winding hillside streets of Launceston through the glorious Cornish countryside—in open carriages on sunny days. The daily ticket allows plenty of opportunity for a meander along the local pathways or a quiet riverside picnic. There's plenty to do at Launceston, with workshops and a museum at the station, and walks over the river to the ancient priory.

LAVENDER LINE

HOW TO FIND US:
By car: Just off the A26
Car parking: On site
By rail: Lewes and Uckfield
By bus: Buses from Lewes and Uckfield stop at the railway
ADDRESS: Isfield Station, Isfield, East Sussex TN22 5XB
TEL: 01825 750 515
LENGTH OF LINE: 1 mile
OPENING TIMES: Sun and bank holidays throughout the year; Sat in July; every day in Aug
FACILITIES: Souvenir shop and café picnic area
DISABLED: Full wheel-chair access.

Named not, as you might expect, because the trains wend their way through scented fields of purple flowers, but after the coal merchants who served the line—A.E.Lavender and Sons. Notwithstanding the lack of flora, this is still well worth a trip. It is part of the former Lewes–Uckfield Railway, which opened in 1858 and ran until 1969. One mile of track has been relaid and the station has been restored to look as it would have done in the 1920s and '30s. There is also a small museum housing various bits of railway paraphernalia in an 1860 Goods Office—the only such office in the country to have been restored and opened to the public.

LEEDS INDUSTRIAL MUSEUM

HOW TO FIND US:
By car: The Armley Mills site is a few miles west of Leeds, just off the A657. It is signposted
Car parking: There is a car park adjacent to the museum
By rail: The nearest mainline station is Leeds, a short bus ride away
By bus: Call Metro 0113 245 7676
ADDRESS: Armley Mills, Canal Road, Leeds LS12 2QF
TEL: 0113 263 7861
OPENING TIMES: 10–4 Tues-Sat; Sun 2–4
FACILITIES: Museum shop, refreshments, picnic area
DISABLED: Wheel-chair access to most areas; adapted toilets

Housed in what was formerly the largest wooden mill in the world, the Leeds Industrial Museum relates the story of the city's proud industrial history. The interior is dominated by the vast clunking, whirring behemoths of the textile industry and there are regular demonstrations of static engines, steam locomotives and underground haulage. Less noisy attractions include a printing gallery and a replica Victorian weaver's cottage. There is also a fully-working recreation of a 1920s cinema. A £10 season ticket gives you unlimited access to all Leeds' principal museums and attractions—including Leeds City Museum, Harewood House and Thackray's medical museum—for a whole year.

LEIGHTON BUZZARD

HOW TO FIND US:
By car: A4146
Car parking: Free
By rail: Leighton Buzzard
By bus: Call 01234 228 337 for details
ADDRESS: Billington Road, Leighton Buzzard, Beds LU7 8TN
TEL: 01525 373 888
WEBSITE: www.btinternet.com/buzzrail
LENGTH OF LINE: 3 miles
OPENING TIMES: Sun and bank holidays mid Mar–early Oct; Wed June–Aug, Thurs in Aug
FACILITIES: Buffet
DISABLED: Wheelchair access

Deepest Bedfordshire, and the largest collection of narrow gauge locomotives in the country is put through its paces along the tight curves and hard climbs of a country-roadside track. Here you can experience the English light railway as it was 80 years ago, with a wide variety of coaches and wagons in use and on display. The railway will celebrate its 80th birthday in 1999, with a special weekend celebration on 27-28 June. There will also be many other special events throughout the year, including a Teddy Bear's outing, the Mad Hatter's Extravaganza and the September Steam-Up.

LIGHTWATER VALLEY

HOW TO FIND US:
By car: A6108
Car parking: Free
By rail: Thirsk
ADDRESS: North Stainley, Ripon, N. Yorkshire HG4 3HT
TEL: 01765 635 368
WEBSITE: www.lightwatervalley.co.uk
OPENING TIMES: W/ends April, May & Oct, every day during school holidays and from June–Aug
FACILITIES: Shopping Centre, various fast food restaurants
DISABLED: Wheelchair access to park; adapted toilets

This jolly miniature steam railway which gently winds its way through Lightwater Valley Theme Park provides welcome relief from the surrounding adrenaline-soaked attractions. The park contains some truly terrifying rides, including 'The Ultimate', the longest rollercoaster in the world; the coiled looping 'Viper'; and 'Sewer Rat', a subterranean rollercoaster. If the railway doesn't calm you down, you can always take a walk through some of the surrounding 175 acres of Yorkshire Dale woodland, or pay a visit to nearby Norton Conyers, a huge imposing medieval house that Charlotte Brontë used as the basis for Thornfield Hall in *Jane Eyre*.

HOW TO FIND US:
By car: Follow signs along B1021
Car parking: Free on site
By rail: Burnham
By bus: Call 0345 000 333
ADDRESS: Southminster Road, Burnham-on-Crouch, Essex CM0 8QQ
TEL: 01621 784 898
LENGTH OF LINE: 0.75 miles
OPENING TIMES: Every w/end and bank holiday except Jan and Feb; every day during school summer holidays
FACILITIES: Refreshments, shop
DISABLED: Limited wheelchair access

This family-run museum on a working farm attempts to summon up the spirit of East Anglian railways past. The historic buildings, moved from various sites in East Anglia and lovingly restored, include a complete working station and signal box; while the museum itself contains one of the largest and most varied collections of railway memorabilia in the country, with signs, notices, posters, nameplates and signalling equipment. In the station yard are various locomotives and wagons ranging from the 1870s to the 1960s. A special attraction is the fascinating collection of relics from the Great Eastern Railway. A 1-mile round trip is also available on the museum's preserved length of track.

HOW TO FIND US:
By car: Off the A31
Car parking: Parking at Alresford and Alton stations
By rail: Alton
By bus: Call 0345 023 067
ADDRESS: Railway Station, Alresford, Hants, SO24 9JG
TEL: 01962 733 810
TALKING TIMETABLE: 01962 734 866
WEBSITE: www.itoeye.co.uk
LENGTH OF LINE: 10 miles
OPENING TIMES: Sun in Feb; w/ends and bank holidays March–Oct; daily July–Aug
FACILITIES: Café book and souvenir shop
DISABLED: Adapted toilets

MID-HANTS

This railway is also known as the 'Watercress Line' because of the watercress beds which still grow in Alresford, a picturesque Georgian town and the railway's headquarters. The journey to Alton is about 10 miles, with two stops on the way. The first, Ropley, the engineering centre of the railway, is famous for its topiary and the site overlooking the station area is a prime spot for photographing the trains or having a picnic. At Medstead and Marks, the highest station in Southern England, you can experience the steep climbs that the crews of yore called going 'Over the Alps'.

MID-NORFOLK

HOW TO FIND US:
By car: Close to centre of Dereham.
Car parking: Free
By rail: Norwich
By bus: Contact Norfolk Bus, 0500 626116
ADDRESS: Railway Station, Station Road, Dereham, Norfolk, NR19 1DF
TEL: 01362 690 633
LENGTH OF LINE: 2 miles (11 miles planned)
OPENING TIMES: Sun all year, some weekdays in summer
FACILITIES: Refreshments and souvenir shop
DISABLED: Wheelchair access

Although the Mid-Norfolk Railway is a relative newcomer to the preserved railway scene, the line itself is over one hundred and fifty years old, and was once part of the Great Eastern Railway network. The aim of the volunteers who recently gathered together to restore the line has been to provide a service and range of exhibits which will appeal to enthusiasts and casual visitors alike. This year the organisers hope to provide a passenger steam service from Dereham to Wymondham, linking numerous villages and passing through four river valleys on the way.

HOW TO FIND US:
By car: Immediately adjacent to Jct 5 of M621
Car parking: Free car park at Moor Road
By rail: Leeds
By bus: Buses run to the station from the Leeds Corn Exchange
ADDRESS: Middleton Railway, Trust Ltd, Moor Road, Leeds LS10 2JQ
TEL: 0113 271 0320
LENGTH OF LINE: 1.25 miles
OPENING TIMES: Sat, Sun & bank holidays April–Oct
FACILITIES: Souvenir shop
DISABLED: Wheelchair access

MIDDLETON

The Middleton Railway holds a number of records: built in 1758, it's one of the oldest railways in the world and the first to be licensed by Parliament. In 1812 it became the first commercially successful steam railway; and in 1960, having closed and fallen into disrepair, it was the first standard gauge railway to be reopened by volunteers. Today, visitors can take a mile-long trip from Moor Road to Middleton Park Halt, where there is a picnic site, a nature trail and a children's playground.

MIDLAND RAILWAY CENTRE

HOW TO FIND US:
By car: 1 mile north of Ripley
Car parking: At Butterley Station
By rail/bus: Derby and then a 91 or 92
ADDRESS: Butterley Station, Ripley, Derbyshire DE5 3TL
TEL: 0773 570140
LENGTH OF LINE: 3.5 miles
OPENING TIMES: W/end and bank holidays throughout the year; Wed from April–Oct; daily in school holidays
FACILITIES: Café, souvenir shops
DISABLED: Wheelchair access to station and coaches; adapted toilets

The Midland Railway Centre celebrated its 25th anniversary in 1998. The huge 57-acre site is constantly acquiring new attractions and is now one of the best equipped railway museums in the country. In its exhibition hall is a collection of locomotives and rolling stock covering the history of rail travel from the 1860s onwards. There's also a miniature railway and a narrow gauge steam line which takes visitors on a trip from Butterley Station to Swanwick Junction. Other exhibits include a demonstration signal box and a restored Victorian railwayman's church.

MOORS VALLEY

HOW TO FIND US:
By car: The railway is on the A31 via Southampton, 3 miles from the ring road
Car parking: On site
By rail: Bournemouth
By bus: X2 stops
ADDRESS: Moors Valley Country Park, Horton Road, Ashley Heath, Ringwood BH21 2ET
TEL: 01425 471 415
LENGTH OF LINE: 1 mile
OPENING TIMES: W/ends March–Oct; daily during school holidays; Sun Nov–Feb
FACILITIES: Buffet, railway, model shop at Kingsmere
DISABLED: Wheelchair access to site but not trains

In the scenic Moors Valley Park, this is the longest fully signalled narrow (7.25") gauge railway in the south of England. The ride takes you past, through and under sharp slopes, tunnels, level crossings, footbridges and signal boxes. There are two stations, Lakeside and Kingsmere, the latter boasting a goods yard, engine shed and workshop. There is also a model shop supplying such names as Hornby, Bachmann and Peco. The park itself features an adventure playground, lakeside picnic areas, 18-hole golf course and forest walks.

MUSEUM OF ARMY TRANSPORT

HOW TO FIND US:
By car: Just off the A164 Hull–Beverley Road;
Car parking: On site
By rail: Beverley
ADDRESS: Museum of Army Transport, Flemingate, Beverley, East Yorkshire HU17 0NG
TEL: 01482 860 445
OPENING TIMES: 10–5 daily
FACILITIES: cafeteria, souvenir shop
DISABLED: Wheelchair access to the floor of the museum, if not all the exhibits; adapted toilets

A huge two-acre hangar full of planes, tanks, jeeps, cars and, of course, trains displayed in various mock-combat settings. You are allowed to clamber inside many of the vehicles, including the museum's largest exhibit, the Blackburn Beverley aircraft. Other items of interest include Montgomery's Rolls Royce, an SAS Pink Panther and an army transport narrow gauge railway; the museum also holds a fascinating archive of army railway memorabilia. Children will enjoy the Sir Patrick Wall model exhibition—over 6,000 beautifully crafted miniature fighting machines—and the junior assault course.

HOW TO FIND US:
By car: The museum is in Castlefield, close to Manchester city centre
Car parking: On-site
By rail: Deansgate
ADDRESS: Liverpool Road, Castlefield, Manchester M3 4FP
TEL: 0161 832 2244
24HR INFO LINE: 0161 832 1830
WEBSITE: www.edes.co.uk.mussci
OPENING TIMES: 10–5 daily
FACILITIES: Coffee shop, café, gift and souvenir shop
DISABLED: 90% wheelchair access, adapted toilets

MUSEUM OF SCIENCE & INDUSTRY

Housed in the world's oldest passenger railway station, next to the Coronation Street set, this enormous museum is crammed full of whirring, buzzing gizmos and gadgets designed to tell the story of one of the world's great industrial cities. There's a four-storey electricity gallery, a fabric and fashion gallery, an air and space gallery with reconstructed biplanes and a rocket simulator, an interactive science gallery—guaranteed to keep children enthralled for hours—and, in the basement, a reconstructed Victorian sewer complete with authentic sounds and smells. On Sundays there are rides on some of the museum's original and replica steam engines, including a version of George Stephenson's 'Planet'—the locomotive which caused the world's first passenger rail death when it backed over Liverpool MP William Huskisson just before its maiden journey.

NATIONAL RAILWAY MUSEUM

HOW TO FIND US:
By car: signed from York's ring road
Car parking: On site
By rail: York
By bus: From York Minster April–Oct,

ADDRESS:
Leeman Road, York YO26 4XJ

TEL: 01904 621 261

WEBSITE:
www.nmsi.ac.uk/nrm

OPENING TIMES:
10–6 daily

FACILITIES: Gift shop, restaurant, cafe

DISABLED:
Wheelchair access to most parts of the museum, wheelchair loan available

This is the largest railway museum in the world, with artefacts, memorabilia and rolling stock from the entire railway age—from Stephenson's Rocket (which will be on display here during 1999 before returning, in 2000, to the Science Museum) to the Eurostar. Its pride and joy, however, is its huge collection of classic steam engines arranged around a 1955 turntable in the Great Hall. You can go inside most, including the Mallard which is the fastest steam locomotive in the world, capable of reaching speeds of up to 126mph. Children are well catered for with Play 'n' Picnic areas, an interactive learning centre and regular visits from Thomas the Tank Engine.

NATIONAL TRAMWAY MUSEUM

HOW TO FIND US:
By car: Crich is just 8 miles from the M1 near Matlock.
Car parking: On site
By rail: Cromford
By bus: local bus times call Busline 01332 292 200

ADDRESS: Crich, Matlock, Derbyshire DE4 5DP

TEL: 01773 852 565

LENGTH OF LINE:
1 mile

OPENING TIMES:
April–Oct: Mon–Fri 10–5.30; Sat, Sun and bank holidays 10–6.30

FACILITIES: Souvenir shop, bookshop, picnic areas

DISABLED: A special access tram has been fitted out to carry people with mobility difficulties

Set in the delightful village of Crich in the heart of the Derbyshire countryside, the National Tramway Museum is the proud owner of the largest collection of preserved trams in Europe—over 70 horse-drawn, steam and electric models gathered from all over the world. When you arrive you are given a vintage penny which you use to pay for your first ride along a one-mile length of track passing through a recreated tram-era street, under the elegant Bowes-Lyon bridge and then out into some wonderful open countryside. Part of the tram line occupies the route of a narrow gauge mineral railway built by George Stephenson. More trams can be found in the large exhibition hall where there is also an interactive display on the history of the tram.

NENE VALLEY

The NVR, one of the country's most famous railways, has been the location for dozens of films and TV programmes, including *Octopussy*, *Goldeneye* and *London's Burning*, and is the home of 'Thomas', perhaps the best loved of all train engines. It recently celebrated its 21st year of operation and today visitors can take a ride starting in Wansford (home to a unique collection of historic European locomotives), passing through scenic Yarwell and on to Orton Mere, where you can alight for a walk in the 500–acre Nene Park, with its model railway circling the central lake, before re-embarking for the final leg to the beautifully restored Peterborough NVR station.

NORTH NORFOLK

The North Norfolk Railway, or 'Poppy Line' as it is affectionately known, is a full-size steam railway running along the beautiful Norfolk coast from the charming Georgian town of Holt to Sheringham, where there is a small steam railway museum. On the way, you can stop off at Weybourne Station, a perfect picnic spot in the middle of some delightful wooded countryside. The Railway also offers trips aboard a sumptuous 1930s Brighton Belle Pullman restaurant car and holds special days when you can learn how to drive a steam engine or operate a signal box.

NORTH WOOLWICH

HOW TO FIND US:
By car: No parking, so travel by alternative means
By rail: North Woolwich
By bus: 69, 101, 473
By boat: Woolwich Free Ferry
ADDRESS:
Pier Road, North Woolwich, London E16 2JJ
TEL: 0171 474 7244
OPENING TIMES:
2–5 Fri & Sun;
10–5 Sat April–Sept;
1–5 Mon–Wed during half term holidays
FACILITIES: Shop
DISABLED: Wheelchair access and adapted toilets

The North Woolwich Old Station Museum offers a revealing glimpse into the golden age of London's railway. It is housed in a very large, very grand Italianate rail terminus, first built in 1847 and restored to its former glory in the '70s and '80s. There are two platforms, a waiting room, a ladies' waiting room and a ticket office, all beautifully recreated with much of the original furniture still in place. Various artefacts relating to the history of rail are on display in replica wooden ticket offices. Outside are several locomotives and carriages from the late 19th and early 20th centuries including a Royal Arsenal Ammunition Wagon.

NORTH YORKSHIRE MOORS

HOW TO FIND US:
By car: Pickering Station is on the A170 between Scarborough and Thirsk
Car parking: At car parks at Pickering, Levisham, Goathland and Grosmont
By rail: Grosmont
ADDRESS: Pickering Station, Pickering, North Yorkshire YO18 7AJ
TEL: 01751 472 508
LENGTH OF LINE:
18 miles
OPENING TIMES:
Daily late March–Oct
FACILITIES:
Refreshments and shops at Pickering, Goathland and Grosmont
DISABLED: Wheelchair access

This was formerly part of the Midland and Great Northern Joint Railway. It runs from Pickering, a lovely Yorkshire market town (the lively street market is held every Monday) set beneath a medieval castle; through Levisham, the gateway to Newton Dale, and its stunning glacial valley; Goathland, the scenic rural village featured in TV's *Heartbeat*; and on to Grosmont, the operational headquarters where various locomotives, including the 1943 Vera Lynn, can be viewed in the engine shed. There are various special events held throughout the year including a Thomas the Tank Engine weekend, a vintage car weekend and brass band concerts in the Levisham Station paddock.

NORTHAMPTON & LAMPORT

HOW TO FIND US:
By car: 5 miles North of Northampton
Car parking: On site.
By rail/bus: Not served by public transport
ADDRESS: Pitsford Road, Chapel Brompton, Northants NN6 8BA
TEL: 01604 820 327
WEBSITE: www.nlr.org.uk
LENGTH OF LINE: 0.75 miles
OPENING TIMES: Diesel service Sun Mar–Nov; steam service Sun & bank holidays April–Oct
FACILITIES: Buffet, souvenir shop
DISABLED: Call ahead

Designed by the two great railway Georges, Bidder and Stephenson, and opened in 1859, the Northampton and Lamport Railway operated as a passenger line for over 120 years. In 1981 work began on its restoration and in 1996 it reopened to the public. Today it is home to a number of steam and diesel locomotives, the oldest built in 1933, which chug up and down a 0.75-mile section of track—work on an extension will begin soon. A country footpath and cycleway runs alongside allowing access to the surrounding countryside.

NORTHANTS IRONSTONE RAILWAY TRUST

HOW TO FIND US:
By car: Just off the M1, 3 miles south of Northampton
Car parking: On site
By rail: Northampton
By bus: no.s 24, 25 and 26
ADDRESS: West Hunsbury, Hunsbury Hill Road, Northampton
TEL: 08024 20985
LENGTH OF LINE: 2.25 miles
OPENING TIMES: Open throughout the year; the railway operates Sun & bank holidays April–Sept as well as Santa Specials in Dec
FACILITIES: Café shop, picnic area and children's play area
DISABLED: Coaches allow wheelchair access

Here, in Northamptonshire's only country park, the relics of the county's ironstone industry have been painstakingly preserved. The ironworks were in existence from 1873 until 1921 when first horses and then steam-powered locomotives pulled wagons full of iron ore along a two-mile quarry side track. The railway was restored in the seventies and a passenger service started in 1982. Further reminders of the grit, grime and grind of yesterday can be found at the railway museum, where there is one of the largest collections of industrial locomotives in the country as well as photographs and documents relating to the history of the ironstone industry.

NOTTS HERITAGE CENTRE

HOW TO FIND US:
By car: 3 miles south of Nottingham
Car parking: On site.
By rail/bus: Nottingham call 0115 924 0000
ADDRESS: Mere Way, Ruddington, Nottingham, NG11 6NX
TEL: 0115 940 5705
LENGTH OF LINE: 2 miles
OPENING TIMES: Open every Sun and bank holiday from mid-April–mid-Oct
FACILITIES: Shop and café, picnic area, country park walks, miniature railways
DISABLED: Wheelchair access

The Great Central Railway operates the only steam railway in Nottinghamshire; a jaunty two-mile ride through Rushcliffe Country Park, from the Heritage Centre itself to 50 Steps Bridge. In 1999 the line should be extended to Rushcliffe Hall, and there are plans afoot to buy a further 5.3 miles of track from Railtrack which would take the railway up to the Stanford Viaduct. At the Heritage Centre, there is an exhibition of vintage buses and a delightful miniature railway. Surrounding it are a network of walks, a wildlife lake and various picnic areas.

PAIGNTON & DARTMOUTH

HOW TO FIND US:
By car: M5, then follow signs for Paignton.
Car parking: Car park in Paignton, and car parks in Goodrington and Kingswear
By rail: Paignton
ADDRESS: Dart Valley Light Railway plc, Queen's Park Station, Paignton, Devon TQ4 6AF
TEL: 01803 553 760
LENGTH OF LINE: 7 miles
OPENING TIMES: Easter–Oct, as well as Santa Specials in Dec
FACILITIES: Refreshment facilities at Paignton and Kingswear
DISABLED: Wheelchair access

To take a trip aboard the Paignton and Dartmouth Steam Railway is to take a step back into a more elegant, refined world. An ideal trip would begin aboard the Riviera Belle Dining Car, sampling its gastronomic delights as you chug along the beautiful Torbay coast from Paignton to the wooded slopes of Kingswear. From here, it's a short ferry journey across the River Dart to historic Dartmouth where you can take a cruise around the harbour, passing the Royal Naval College, Bayard's Cove and Dartmouth castle, or along the river itself to Totnes in the heart of the English Riviera.

PEAK RAILWAY

Until 1968, when the St Pancras–Manchester express route was terminated and the track torn up, Midland Railway operated one of the best-loved steam routes in the country, through the heart of Derbyshire's Peak District. Since the late 1960s Peak Rail has been working towards restoring and reopening the most scenic part of the line, between Buxton and Matlock. Thus far 4.5 miles of track and three stations (Matlock, Darley Dale and Rowsley) are in operation. How you travel is up to you: you can sit and admire the wonderful rolling countryside from the refined surroundings of the Palatine restaurant coaches or take a more hands-on approach in the earthier atmosphere of the locomotive engine itself—the railway runs courses for people to learn how to drive and fire a locomotive.

PERRYGROVE

The Perrygrove Railway is best described as a cross between a miniature railway and a full-blown steam railway—a sort of teenage railway—and, as a result, is hugely popular with children and adults alike. Although the train runs on 15" gauge track, the engine is still large enough to allow the driver to stand upright; this is the only locomotive of its kind where the driver can do this. The track itself, laid out on the edge of the beautiful forest of Dean, is currently 0.75 miles long, although there are plans for a further 0.25-mile extension.

HOW TO FIND US:
By car: 5 miles from Plymouth centre
Car parking: On-site
By rail: Plymouth
By bus: no.s 20, 20A, 21, 22A and 51 run from Plymouth
ADDRESS: Marsh Mills Station, Coypool Road, Marsh Mills, Plymouth, Devon PL7 4NL
TEL: 01503 250 539
LENGTH OF LINE: 0.5 miles
OPENING TIMES: Limited Sun service
FACILITIES: Shop and refreshments at Marsh Mills station
DISABLED: Wheelchair access to platform and trains

The Plym Valley Railway is a reconstruction of part of the former Great Western Railway's Tavistock branch which ran through some delightful leafy Devon countryside. So far, a new station, locomotive shed and sidings have been built and half a mile of track relaid. The aim is to reopen the 1.5 miles of track from Marsh Mills to Plym Bridge, and it is hoped a Sunday service will begin operating in early 1999, using a wide variety of steam and diesel locomotives including Falmouth Docks No.3—the last steam locomotive to be in industrial use in Southwest England.

RAVENGLASS

HOW TO FIND US:
By car: A595 coast road between Barrow-in-Furness and Whitehaven
Car parking: On site
By rail: Ravenglass.
ADDRESS: Ravenglass, Cumbria CA18 1SW
TEL: 01229 717 171
LENGTH OF LINE: 7 miles
OPENING TIMES: Daily late March–Oct; winter service Nov–Mar, call ahead
FACILITIES: Pub, railway museum at Ravenglass, souvenir shop and café in Eskdale
DISABLED: Wheelchair access to some coaches; adapted toilets

Originally built to carry iron ore from mines in Eskdale, the Ravenglass and Eskdale Railway, known locally as La'al Ratty, is today one of the most popular tourist lines in the country. The journey begins at Ravenglass, home to a first-century Roman bathouse, passing through Muncaster with its medieval castle and 15th-century working water-mill, and then out into the rich Cumbrian countryside of rugged mountains, dry stone walls, crystal-clear rivers and waterfalls, before coming to rest at Eskdale, site of the famous Hardknott Fort, built by the Romans in *c.* 100 BC.

ROMNEY, HYTHE & DYMCHURCH

HOW TO FIND US:
By car: Hythe Station is just 3 miles from the M20, Jct 11.
Car parking: On site
By rail/bus: Folkestone Central, then bus to Hythe
ADDRESS: New Romney Station, Kent TN28 8PL
TEL: 01797 362 353
WEBSITE: www.i-way.co.uk\ tburgess\rhdr.html\ rhdr.

LENGTH OF LINE: 13.5 miles
FACILITIES: Cafés and souvenir shops
DISABLED: Wheelchair access on trains, but call in advance; adapted

The Romney, Hythe and Dymchurch Railway is a true historical oddity; a 0.35-size miniature railway built in the 1920s for the racing car driver Captain Howey, who hoped to operate it as a full mainline railway carrying freight as well as passengers. Unfortunately for the Captain, British industry didn't share his vision and it was forced to rely on holidaymakers for its main source of income. It fell into disrepair in World War II, but was restored and reopened in 1946 (at a ceremony attended by Laurel and Hardy). Today, it can claim the honour of being the world's longest 15" gauge railway, running for 13.5 miles across Romney Marsh from Hythe to Dungeness, passing through New Romney, with its famous Toy and Model Museum, on the way.

ROYAL VICTORIA

HOW TO FIND US:
By car: Brown tourist signs from Jct 8 off M27 or A27
Car parking: Four free car parks in the Royal Victoria Country Park
By rail: Netley
ADDRESS: Royal Victoria Country Park, Netley SO31 5GA
TEL: 01703 456246
LENGTH OF LINE: 1 mile
OPENING TIMES: Every w/end and school holidays from 11.30am onwards
FACILITIES: Tea rooms and picnic areas in the park
DISABLED: Wheelchair access; a special leaflet for the disabled is available on request,

This sprightly and colourful miniature railway was built in 1995 and operates around a 1-mile circuit in the Royal Victoria Country Park—there are plans for a further 0.5 mile extension. It is aimed principally at children—the line circles a children's play area and all the engines have cute names such as Maurice the Major—but adults will be able to appreciate the glorious country park setting overlooking Southampton Water. Nearby, in the country park, a 100ft tower offers some stupendous panoramic views of the Hampshire countryside and out over the sea to the Isle of Wight.

RUTLAND RAILWAY MUSEUM

HOW TO FIND US:
By car: 4 miles north of Oakham between Ashwell and Cottesmore
Car parking: On-site
By rail: Oakham
ADDRESS: Ashwell Road, Cottesmore, Oakham, Rutland LE15 7BX
TEL: 01572 813 203
LENGTH OF LINE: 0.75 miles
OPENING TIMES: W/ends 11–5 throughout the year
FACILITIES: Refreshments, picnic sites, shop
DISABLED: No facilities

In the late 19th century and for much of the 20th, iron ore mining was one of Rutland's principal industries and Cottesmore home to one of its most successful quarries. When the quarry closed in 1973, a group of railway enthusiasts gathered together in order to preserve and restore what remained of the county's industrial legacy. Today, the Rutland Railway Museum's collection of quarry stock is probably the most comprehensive in the country. Its showpiece is a 0.75 mile line relaid on the former quarry route where, on 'Steam Days', you have the opportunity to ride aboard a restored quarry locomotive.

Cottesmore itself enjoys an idyllic setting between Rutland Water and the picturesque village of Stamford recently featured in the BBC series *Middlemarch*.

SEATON TRAMWAY

HOW TO FIND US:
By car: Seaton is on the A358
Car parking: On site
By rail/bus: Axminster from where there is a bus
ADDRESS: Harbour Road, Seaton, Devon EX12 2NQ
TEL: 01297 20375
WEBSITE: http://members.aol.com-seatrams
LENGTH OF LINE: 3 miles
OPENING TIMES: Daily Mar–Oct; W/ends Nov–Xmas
FACILITIES: Gift shops, tea rooms, children's playground, picnic areas
DISABLED: One tram has been specially adapted for wheelchair use

A ride aboard a Seaton tram is a wonderful way of exploring the quaint, homely villages and rich green countryside of the Axe Valley. The electric tramway runs for three miles alongside the River Axe (home to a variety of wading birds including oyster catchers, shelduck and grey heron) from Seaton to Colyton via Colyford—the tramway shop at Colyton is an original 1868 railway building. All the trams are purpose-built half-size versions of the trams that ran in Britain's towns and cities before World War II. Tram driving lessons are offered every Friday and Saturday during the season.

SEVERN VALLEY

HOW TO FIND US:
By car: Bridgnorth is
on the A458
Car parking: On site
By rail:
Kidderminster
ADDRESS:
The Railway Station,
Bewdley,
Worcs DY12 1BG
TEL: 01299 403 816
WEBSITE:
www.svr.co.uk
LENGTH OF LINE:
16.5 miles
OPENING TIMES:
Every w/end from
late May–early Oct
FACILITIES: Buffet
and bar facilities,
station bars, tea
rooms, gift shops
DISABLED: Specially
converted carriages
are available

The Severn Valley Railway not only has more mainline engines that any other preserved railway in the country but, at over 16 miles, also has one of the longest lines. The railway starts at Bridgnorth, a bustling market town and recent winner of the 'Britain in Bloom' competition, and stops off at Hamton Loade, from where you can take a walk to Dudnaston Hall with its extensive landscaped gardens, and Bewdley, which has been described as 'simply the most beautiful town in England'. The final stop is Kidderminster, where there is a small Railway Museum.

SITTINGBOURNE

HOW TO FIND US:
By car: A2 between
Gillingham and
Canterbury
Car parking: On site
By rail:
Sittingbourne
ADDRESS:
Sittingbourne &
Kemsley Light
Railway Ltd, PO Box
300, Sittingbourne,
Kent ME10 2DZ
TEL: 01634 852 672
TALKING TIMETABLE:
01795 424 899
WEBSITE: www.sklr.
demon.co.uk
LENGTH OF LINE:
2 miles
OPENING TIMES:
Sun & bank holidays
Easter–early Oct;
Wed and Sat in Aug
FACILITIES: Shop,
café, picnic area
DISABLED: No
wheelchair access

A relic of Kent's still-flourishing paper industry, the railway was built in 1906 to carry paper between the mills of Sittingbourne and Kemsley to the Docks at Ridham on the banks of the Swale. Two of the original engines are still in use today. Besides being a fascinating historical monument, the Sittingbourne railway also offers delightful scenic rides through the picnic-perfect Kent countryside. The railway holds various special events throughout the year including a 'Steam and Beer' festival and a model railway exhibition.

SOMERSET & DORSET RAILWAY TRUST

This fascinating museum and photo-graphic archive was set up by railway enthusiasts dedicated to preserving the memory of the great Somerset and Dorset Railway, which ran from 1862 until 1966. There is a vast horde of memorabilia and artefacts on display which helps to paint a vivid picture of one of Britain's best-loved railways. Visitors can watch locomotive wagons and carriages being restored In the engine shed or pull the levers in the recon-structed Midford Signal Box. The Trust organises various annual events including a model railway exhibition, track bed walks and film shows.

SOUTH DEVON

The South Devon Railway or 'Primrose Line' is one of the best railways in the country for observing and encountering wildlife. It starts at Totnes and runs for seven miles along the East bank of the River Dart—a fast-flowing salmon river, home to herons, swans and kingfishers. At the terminus at Buckfastleigh, you can watch otters swimming and playing from an underwater viewing gallery at the Otter Sanctuary or walk through clouds of free-flying tropical butterflies at the associated Butterfly Park. Nearby is Buckfast Abbey, one of the most visited religious institutions in the country and the source of an internationally renowned brand of honey. The railway also offers combined railway-river cruise tickets.

SOUTH TYNEDALE

HOW TO FIND US:
By car: Alston Station is just off the A686 Hexham Road
Car parking: On site
By rail: Haltwhistle
By bus: Bus service running from Durham
ADDRESS:
The Railway Station, Alston, Cumbria CA9 3JB
TEL: 01434 381 696
TALKING TIMETABLE: 01434 382 828
LENGTH OF LINE: 2.25 miles
OPENING TIMES: W/ends April–Oct; daily in July and Aug,
FACILITIES: Tea room
DISABLED: A carriage with wheelchair access is available

The journey on England's highest narrow gauge railway begins in Alston, just 20 miles south of Hadrian's Wall, and continues through some beautiful North Pennine scenery to Kirkhaugh. The line was constructed on the trackbed of the former BR Haltwhistle–Alston branch and, it is hoped, will soon be extended to Slaggyford. Alston itself, a pleasant cobbled village, was once the centre of an important lead-mining district. You can find out more about the area's rich industrial heritage at the nearby Nenthead Mines Heritage Centre.

SPA VALLEY

HOW TO FIND US:
By car: Tunbridge Wells West is just off the A26 Tunbridge Wells–Crowborough Road
Car parking: Nearby in town
By rail: Tunbridge Wells
ADDRESS: West Station, Tunbridge Wells, Kent TN4 8HL
TEL: 01892 537 715
WEBSITE: www.ucl.ac.uk/pers/1278/rlypres/spa.html
LENGTH OF LINE: 3 miles
OPENING TIMES: W/ends April–Oct; Wed–Fri from mid July–Aug; Christmas Specials
FACILITIES: Café and souvenir shop at Tunbridge West
Disabled: No specific facilities

The much-loved Tunbridge Wells–Edridge line was in operation as a passenger service from the mid-nineteenth century until 1985. In 1996, after much work by a preservation society, it was reopened to the public as a steam railway. At present, the line runs from Tunbridge to Groombridge—home of Groombridge Gardens—but the society hopes to extend the line soon to the halt at High Rocks and eventually to Edridge. The engine shed at Tunbridge (built in 1891) contains various fascinating examples of rolling stock.

SWANAGE RAILWAY

HOW TO FIND US:
By car: On the A351
Car parking: On site
By rail: Wareham
By bus: From
Wareham Station
ADDRESS: Southern
Steam Trust, Station
House, Swanage,
Dorset BH19 1HB
TEL: 01929 425 800
WEBSITE: www.swan
rail.demon.co.uk/
LENGTH OF LINE:
6 miles
OPENING TIMES:
W/ends and school
holidays through the
year; daily April–Oct;
Specials in Dec
FACILITIES: Souvenir
shop, station buffet
DISABLED: Wheel-
chair access onto
trains

Swanage, a sleepy Dorset coastal resort, is the starting point for the Purbeckline, one of the west country's most picturesque steam railways. The line runs all the way to Norden but there is an opportunity to get off and explore the ruins of the famous Corfe Castle en route. A Royalist stronghold during the civil war, the castle withstood a Cromwellian siege for six weeks, after which it was largely reduced to rubble by Round-head gunpowder. At Swanage Station there is an exhibition of railway memorablia and an engine shop where you can take a closer look at locomotives in various states of disrepair.

SWINDON & CRICKLADE RAIL SOCIETY

HOW TO FIND US:
By car: 2 miles NW
of Swindon, near the
A419 off the M4
Car parking: Tadpole
Lane, Blunsdon
By rail: Swindon
ADDRESS: Blunsdon
Station, Blunsdon,
Swindon, Wiltshire
SN2 4DZ
TEL: 01793 771 615
LENGTH OF LINE:
1 mile
OPENING TIMES:
Sat and Sun
throughout year
FACILITIES: Museum,
gift shop and café
DISABLED: Limited
wheelchair access,
call ahead

The Swindon and Cricklade Rail Society was formed in 1978 with the intention of rebuilding and restoring part of the then defunct Midland and South Western Junction Railway. Eventually, they hope to relay four miles of track and rebuild the accompanying signal boxes, engine sheds and stations. Thus far, one mile of track, two steam locomotives and two stations are in operation. Every weekend visitors are invited to come and experience a recreated idyll from steam's golden age: gently puffing trains, whirring signal boxes and quiet rural stations. If you want you can even join in—help with painting fences, restoring rolling stock or learn how to drive and fire an engine.

TANFIELD RAILWAY

HOW TO FIND US:
By car: Off the A6076
Car parking: On site
By rail: Newcastle
By bus: X30 from Newcastle
ADDRESS: Marley Hill Engine Shed, Sunniside, Gateshead.
TEL: 0191 274 2002
WEBSITE: www.tanfield-railway. freeserve.co.uk/dev_ index.html
LENGTH OF LINE: 3 miles
OPENING TIMES: Trains run every Sun throughout the year
FACILITIES: Most trains have a buffet car, railway shop
DISABLED: Manual wheelchair access to some carriages

Built in 1725 to carry coal from Newcastle's mines to the ships on the Tyne, this is the oldest surviving railway in the world. Steam trains still operate along a three-mile length of track passing through Causey Woods, site of Causey Arch, the world's earliest railway bridge. Tanfield's oldest surviving building is the 1844 Marley Hill engine shed, where visitors can watch the ongoing restoration of engines—there is often a blacksmith on hand, forging new parts in the traditional manner. In winter, kids will enjoy the special North Pole days when the trains puff through the beautiful winter landscape on their way to see Santa.

VINTAGE CARRIAGES TRUST MUSEUM

HOW TO FIND US:
By car: On the A629 between Keighley and Skipton
Car parking: On site;
By rail: Ingrow West
ADDRESS: Ingrow Station Yard, Halifax Road, Keighley, West Yorkshire BD21 5AZ
TEL: 01535 680 425
OPENING TIMES: 11.30–5 daily
FACILITIES: Refreshments, museum shop
DISABLED: Wheelchair access, stairlift, adapted toilets; braille leaflet, guidebook and audio tape available; special facilities for visitors with hearing difficulties

A prop man's dream, the museum's exhibits have been featured in more than 30 films and TV programmes including *The Secret Agent* and *The Railway Children*. It houses a huge collection of beautifully restored late 19th and early 20th century locomotives and carriages—a particular highlight is the prize-winning 1876 Manchester, Sheffield & Lincolnshire Railway carriage. There is also a two-hour video presentation. To see trains in action visit the nearby Keighley & Worth Valley Railway (*see* p.25). Also worth a detour is Cliffe Castle Museum and Gallery, a 19th-century country mansion containing various items of furniture from the V&A Museum in London.

WELLS & WALSINGHAM

HOW TO FIND US:
By car: Just off the A149
By bus: Eastern Counties Buses
ADDRESS: Wells Next-the-Sea, Norfolk NR23 1QB.
TEL: 01328 710631
TALKING TIMETABLE: 01328 710 631
LENGTH OF LINE: 4 miles
OPENING TIMES: Daily Easter–Sept
FACILITIES: Refreshments

This is the longest 10.25″ narrow gauge steam railway in the world. It runs from the lively North Norfolk harbour town of Wells to Walsingham, the site of a famous Augustinian Priory which, for many centuries, was as popular a centre of pilgrimage as Canterbury. Much of the Abbey was destroyed in the 16th century following Henry VIII's theological breach with Rome, but you can still visit its evocative remains and the pleasant surrounding gardens and woodland. Nearby, the Shirehall Museum houses a restored Georgian courtroom. You can stand in the dock, sit on the judge's chair or even visit the cells before returning to Wells, where refreshments are served in a converted signal box.

WEST LANCASHIRE LIGHT RAILWAY

HOW TO FIND US:
By car: Between Preston and Southport
Car parking: On site.
By rail: Preston and Southport.
By bus: Nos 100 & 102
ADDRESS: Alty's Brickworks, Station Road, Hesketh Bank, near Preston, Lancs
TEL: 01772 815 881
OPENING TIMES: Every Sun and bank holiday Easter–Oct
FACILITIES: Refreshments, picnic table, souvenir shop
DISABLED: Call ahead

In the 1950s and '60s, Britain's narrow gauge railways, formerly popular forms of transport for the agricultural, mining and building industries, began disappearing as the country's road net-

work was expanded. The West Lancashire Railway was founded with the intention of gathering and preserving as much as remained of these delightful little railways before they vanished for ever. It has a huge collection of railway equipment gathered from all parts of the country. The highlight is undoubtedly the railway line itself, which runs from Hesketh Bank near Preston to Southport. The carriages are often pulled by the railway's pride and joy, a 1898 Hunslet steam engine called Jonathan.

HOW TO FIND US:
By car: Bishops Lydeard station is 4 miles from Taunton
Car parking: On site
By rail: Taunton
By bus: 28A
ADDRESS: Minehead, Somerset TA24 5BG
TEL: 01643 704996
TALKING TIMETABLE: 01643 707650
WEBSITE: www. West-Somerset Railway.co.uk
OPENING TIMES: March through to Jan
LENGTH OF LINE: 20 miles
FACILITIES: Buffet, souvenir shops and buffet car on most trains
DISABLED: Wheelchair access to all stations except Doniford Halt

This charming recreation of a Great Western Railways country branch line is Britain's longest preserved railway. It runs from Bishops Lydeard to Minehead, passing the renowned Quantock Hills and Bristol Channel en route. You may also recognise the immaculately restored station at Crowcombe Heathfield from its numerous film and television appearances. There are museums and displays of engines and stock at Williton, Washford, Blue Anchor and Minehead, whilst Stogumber, Watchet and Dunster are as picturesque as they are historical, with plenty of likely picnic spots on the beach or in the surrounding countryside.

ALFORD VALLEY

HOW TO FIND US:
By car: Alford is located on the A944, 25 miles west of Aberdeen
Car parking: On site
By rail/bus: Aberdeen. Buses operate services from there to Alford,
ADDRESS: Alford, Aberdeenshire AB33 8AD
TEL: 01975 562 326
LENGTH OF LINE: Nearly 2 miles
OPENING TIMES: W/ends in April, May, Sept and Oct; daily June–Aug
FACILITIES: Picnic area
DISABLED: Wheelchair access

During the late 19th century the Alford Valley branch line was the focus of a thriving agricultural and granite-quarrying region. The station builiding, around which the town of Alford grew up, is now the headquarters of the new Alford Valley Railway. From here the line heads north into the grounds of Haughton House, one of the largest estates in the district, and through the beautiful natural woodland of Murray Park. Engines include the steam locomotive 'Saccharine' named in honour of its years spent working on a sugar plantation (not in Aberdeenshire).

BO'NESS & KINNEIL RAILWAY MUSEUM

HOW TO FIND US:
By car: Bo'ness is on the A904
Car parking: On site
By rail: Linlithgow and Falkirk
By bus: Call 01324 613 777
ADDRESS: Union Street, Bo'ness, West Lothian, EH51 9AQ
TEL: 01506 822 298
LENGTH OF LINE: 3.5 miles
OPENING TIMES: W/ends April–Oct; daily July–Aug (except Mon); Specials in Dec
FACILITIES: Shop, buffet/restaurant, baby-changing facilities, buffet car on some trains
DISABLED: Wheelchair access

The Bo'ness and Kinneil Railway Museum aims to give a complete historical overview of the development of the Scottish railway. There is a huge purpose-built exhibition hall in which Scotland's largest collection of locomotives and rolling stock is displayed, as well as various railway buildings relocated from sites all over Scotland. The seven-mile round trip on the railway itself takes passengers through the ancient woodland of the Avon Gorge, home to a variety of native wildlife including deer and otters. Also on the Kinneil Estate are the remains of a small Roman fortt and the workshop where James Watt developed the steam engine.

This last remaining section of the former Caledonian Railway branch line runs from Brechin Station, the line's only extant terminus and home to a small railway museum, to Bridge of Dun, a good base for walks along the River Esk to the Montrose Basin bird sanctuary. Also in the vicinity is the House of Dun, an early 18th-century building owned and run by the National Trust for Scotland. Currently one steam and three diesel locomotives are in service on the line.

GLASGOW MUSEUM OF TRANSPORT

The history of transport, from horse-drawn carriages to high-speed trains, is told in this fantastic museum in Glasgow's twin-towered Kelvin Hall. Its collection of railway locomotives and stock is among the very finest in Europe. There's a recreated 1950s cobbled street scene, with period shops and an underground station as well as a cinema showing archive film of trams and trains crammed full of Glaswegians on their way to the sea. In the Clyde Room there are models of every ship forged on the famous docks.

LEADHILLS AND WANLOCKHEAD

HOW TO FIND US:
By car: Between
Clydesdale (M74)
and Nithsdale (A76).
Car parking: On site
By rail/bus:
Sanquhar. Bus
services run from
the station
ADDRESS: c/o
Douglas Boyd, The
Saltings, Battlehill,
Annan DG12 6SN
TEL: 01461 202 422
LENGTH OF LINE:
1 mile
OPENING TIMES:
Easter w/end; every
w/end and bank
holiday May–Sept,
Facilities: Shop,
picnic area
Disabled: No wheel-
chair access

Built on part of a former Caledonian Railways branch line some 4.900 feet above sea level, this is the highest adhesion railway in Britain. It runs from Leadhills,where, in the local cemetery, you can find an obelisk commemorating William Symington and his contribution to steam navigation (as well as the tombstone of William Taylor, 137 when he died), to Wanlockhead. There are museums at either end containing, respectively, a collection of loco-motives from all over the world and an exhibition detailing the history of the region's lead-mining industry.

HOW TO FIND US:
By ferry: Caledonian
Macbrayne. Call
0990 650 000
By car: At Craignure
Ferry Terminal, turn
left along the A849
and follow signs
By rail: Oban, take
the ferry from there
Car parking: Free at
Craignure station
ADDRESS: Craignure,
Isle of Mull,
PA65 6AY
TEL: 01680 812 494
WEBSITE:www.zynet.
co.uk/ mull/rail
LENGTH OF LINE:
1.25 miles
OPENING TIMES:
April–mid-Oct
FACILITIES: Small
shop at Craignure
station
DISABLED: Wheel-
chair access to both
stations; specially
adapted carriage

MULL & WEST HIGHLAND

Scotland's first island passenger railway is served by three steam engines, 'Lady of the Isles', 'Waverley' and 'Victoria'. From the Old Pier Station at Craignure the trains climb up to the stately home of Torosay Castle where there are beautiful panoramic views of Ben Nevis, the Glencoe Hills, the Island of Lismore, and Duart Castle. The island itself is still largely unspoilt and is teeming with natural wonders—over eighty species of bird have been spotted, and primroses, wild garlic, rhododendrons, orchids and butterflies flourish in the spring and summer.

SCOTTISH INDUSTRIAL RAILWAY CENTRE

HOW TO FIND US:
By car: On the A713
Car parking: On-site
By rail: Ayre
By bus: No. 51 from the station
ADDRESS:
Dalmellington,
Ayrshire KA6 7JF
TEL: 01292 531 144
WEBSITE:
www.btconnect.
com/dunaskin
OPENING TIMES:
Sat June–Sept;
Steam Days run
some Suns between
May and Sept
FACILITIES:
Buffet, book and
souvenir shop
DISABLED: Wheel-
chair access to
Centre and trains

Built on the site of the old Minnevey Colliery, the centre celebrates the rich tradition of ironworking and coal mining in the area and, in particular, the role played by the railways in the development of these industries. The Dalmellington Iron Company began operations at Dunaskin in 1845, and Minnevey was part of the network of industrial railways that supplied coal for the ironworks—there were steam trains running here as late as 1978. Guided tours round the centre relate the history of the railways, and visitors can also see a collection of memorabilia in the small museum. On steam days there is a passenger service between the Centre and Dunaskin Heritage Park.

HOW TO FIND US:
By car: Aviemore
and Boat of Garten
are both just off the
B970
Car parking: On site
By rail: Aviemore
ADDRESS:
Strathspey Steam
Railway, Dalfaber
Road, Aviemore
PH22 1PY
TEL: 01479 810 725
LENGTH OF LINE:
5.5 miles
OPENING TIMES:
Sat from early April
to Oct
FACILITIES:
Refreshments at
stations, buffet car
on most trains,
souvenir shops
DISABLED: Wheel-
chair access to both
stations

STRATHSPEY

A wonderful trip past heather-clad hills, mist-covered lochs and fast running streams on Scotland's premier Highland railway. It runs from the modern skiing resort of Aviemore to the traditional country village of Boat of Garten, just over five miles away. Here, at a viewing site three miles from the station, you have the opportunity to catch a glimpse of one of Scotland's few remaining breeding pairs of ospreys. Perhaps the best way to appreciate the stunning scenery is aboard the restaurant car—formerly a carriage on the 'Flying Scotsman'—sampling the delicious local fare. You can also go monster-hunting at Loch Ness, just 20 miles away.

SUMMERLEE HERITAGE PARK

HOW TO FIND US:
By car: M8 then exit at Jct 8, follow signs to Coatbridge. From the west, take the A8 and follow the signs towards Coatbridge
Car parking: On site
By rail: Coatbridge Sunnyside and Coatbridge Central
ADDRESS: Heritage Way, Coatbridge, ML5 1QD
TEL: 01236 431 261
OPENING TIMES: Daily throughout the year
FACILITIES: Gallery, café, gift shop
DISABLED: Wheelchair access to most areas

This 22-acre site holds a fascinating collection of railway stock and artefacts designed to illustrate West Scotland's rich industrial heritage. It has Scotland's only working electric tramway, a recreated mine which graphically displays the dirt and dangers faced by miners in the days of the pick and shovel, and various locomotives and engines from around the world. A few minutes walk away is the Monklands Canal, once a key industrial artery linking the factories and mines of Glasgow to the sea.

GROUDLE GLEN

HOW TO FIND US:
By ferry: Services from Morecambe, call 01524 853 802
By car: 2.5 miles from Douglas
Car parking: At the beach
By tram: MER trams
ADDRESS:
29 Hawarden Avenue, Douglas, Isle of Man IM1 4BP
TEL: 01624 622 138
LENGTH OF LINE:
0.75 miles
OPENING TIMES:
Sun and bank holidays May–Sept
FACILITIES:
Gift shop, light refreshments
DISABLED: Limited wheelchair access, call in advance

Groudle Glen was orginally built to indulge the Victorian holidaymaker's penchant for seaside vacations. Today, over a century later, visitors can still appreciate the same spectacular setting and stimulating airs. The original locomotive, 'Sea Lion', is once again steaming its way out of the leafy glen towards some dramatic cliff-top views. The journey passes enclosures which once housed sea lions and polar bears as well as a distinctive rebuilt 'Swiss chalet' canopy building at Lhen Coan.

ISLE OF MAN STEAM RAILWAY

HOW TO FIND US:
By ferry: Services from Morecambe, call 01524 853 802
By car: At Douglas Harbour
Car parking: Douglas
By bus:
Tel: 01624 663 366
ADDRESS: Strathallan Crescent, Douglas, Isle of Man, IM2 4NR
LENGTH OF LINE:
15.5 miles
OPENING TIMES:
Easter–Autumn
FACILITIES:
Refreshments and souvenir shops at Douglas and Port Erin. There is also a museum at Port Erin
Disabled: Wheelchair access throughout Douglas and Port Erin stations

The longest narrow gauge steam railway in the British Isles takes the traveller on a journey past magnificent coastal views, through charming woodlands and over picturesque hedged meadows to Port Erin. Its flagship locomotive is 'Loch', which opened the line in 1874 and is still hauling passengers to this day—one of the oldest steam engines in service in the world. The line passes through several beautiful Victorian stations at Douglas, Castletown and Port St Mary. 1999 will be a particularly good year to visit the line as Port Erin celebrates its 125th year of steam travel.

MANX ELECTRIC RAILWAY

HOW TO FIND US:
By ferry: Services from Morecambe, call 01524 853 802
By car: On the Douglas promenade,
Car parking: On site
By bus:
Call 01624 663 366
TEL: 01624 663 366
ADDRESS: Strathallan Crescent, Douglas, Isle of Man IM2 4NR
LENGTH OF LINE:
17.75 miles
OPENING TIMES:
Daily Easter–Oct
FACILITIES:
Refreshments, souvenir shop
DISABLED: Folded wheelchairs can be carried, please call in advance

Another Manx Victorian survivor, the railway was built in 1893 and still employs two of its original cars—making them the oldest regularly operating electric tram cars in the world. The line starts on the coast, from where it heads inland to explore glens, hills, and picturesque villages. It stops at many places of interest including the famous wheel at Laxey, the fascinating village of Maughold (alight at Ballajora) with its ancient church and Celtic crosses, and Ramsey, the island's northern 'capital' ,where there is a small railway museum. The line provides access to many beautiful walks in the glens and woods of the island.

SNAEFELL MOUNTAIN RAILWAY

HOW TO FIND US:
By ferry: Services from Morecambe, call 01524 853 802
By car: Douglas to Ramsey Coast Road
Car parking: On site
By rail: Laxey Station is served by the Manx Electric Railway (see above)
By bus: The Isle of Man Transport Bus goes to Laxey
TEL: 01624 663 366
ADDRESS: Strathallan Crescent, Douglas, Isle of Man IM2 4NR
LENGTH OF LINE:
4.5 miles
OPENING TIMES:
Daily, May–Sept
FACILITIES:
Refreshments at Laxey, Summit café, souvenir shop
DISABLED:
No special wheel-chair facilities

It is 6,560 feet to the top of Snaefell, and there are two ways to get there. You can walk, which would take you the best part of a day, or you can choose the more leisurely option aboard the Mountain Railway. The six original tram cars, built in 1895, still climb the 1 in 12 gradient and provide wonderful panoramic views over the island's valleys, cliffs and plains. According to Manx tradition the summit affords views of six kingdoms. The first five are England, Ireland, Scotland, Wales and Mann. The sixth is somewhat harder to perceive—it is the Kingdom of God, and is only visible to those whose eyes are clear of hate and full of love.

HOW TO FIND US:
By car: Just off the A494 Bala to Dollgellau road
Car parking: On site
By rail: Barmouth and Wrexham
By bus: No. 94 runs from Barmouth
ADDRESS:
The Station, Llanuwchllyn, Gwynedd LL23 7DD
TEL: 01678 540 666
LENGTH OF LINE: 4.5 miles
OPENING TIMES: Mid-April to the beginning of Oct
FACILITIES: Refreshments and souvenir shop
DISABLED: Facilities available on most trains

This dapper little line, built to link the industrial borderlands with the Cambrian coastal resorts, runs along the shoreline of Wales' largest natural lake. The ride offers unforgettable views of deep river valleys, tranquil water meadows, sheep-dotted hill-sides and, of course, the majestic splendour of Bala Lake itself. The headquarters at Llanuwchllyn features an original Great Western signal box, while the main inter-mediate station, at pretty Llangower, is a popular picnic and walking spot. The more active among you may like to try the range of watersports available at Bala Lake.

BRECON MOUNTAIN

HOW TO FIND US:
By car: Pant Station is in Merthyr Tydfil
Car parking: Onsite
By rail: Merthyr
By bus: 30 and 31 run from Merthyr bus station to Pant Cemetery
ADDRESS: Pant Station, Dowlais, Merthyr Tydfil CF48 2UP
TEL: 01685 722 988
LENGTH OF LINE: 3.5 miles
OPENING TIMES: Open most days from end of April–Sept, some days in Oct
FACILITIES: Café at Pant, snack-bar at Pontsticill
DISABLED: Wheelchair-adapted carriage, ramps, adapted toilets

Built on the trackbed of the former Brecon & Methyr Railway, this narrow gauge passenger-carrying steam railway winds its way through the beautiful Brecon Beacons National Park in South Wales. You can watch old steam locomotives being repaired in the station workshop, take a picnic overlooking the magnificent Taf Fechan Reservoir or pay a visit to Cyfarthfa Castle, a splendid Regency Gothic mansion set in wonderful manicured gardens.

This friendly, cheerful museum holds a fascinating collection of railway stock and memorabilia including various model train layouts. There's a mile-long miniature railway and a 15" Tramway available daily for passenger rides. Nearby attractions include Dolwyddelan Castle, the reputed birthplace of Llewelyn the Great, and the picturesque towns of Llanrwst and Penmachno, the last home to a working water mill.

CORRIS RAILWAY MUSEUM

The museum's displays have been designed to explain the history of the old Corris Railway, the first narrow gauge line in Mid-Wales, originally built to transport slate from the quarries of the Dulas Valley to quays on the River Dovey. Later it became a hugely popular tourist line and within the museum are the remains of one of the carriages which once helped carry over 80,000 Victorian holiday-makers a year to the Lake of Talyllyn and the mountain massif of Cadair Idris. There are photographs showing the old trains climbing up through the wooded Dulas valley as well as models of the railway's buildings and rolling stock. The line should open to passenger traffic again in the near future.

FAIRBOURNE & BARMOUTH

HOW TO FIND US:
By car: On the A493, 7 miles south west of Dolgellal
Car parking: Gorsaf Newydd
By rail: Fairbourne
By bus: no. 28
ADDRESS:
Beach Road, Fairbourne, Gwynedd LL38 2PZ
TEL: 01341 250 362
LENGTH OF LINE:
2.5 miles
OPENING TIMES:
April–Oct, Santa Specials
FACILITIES: Souvenir shop and tea shop at Fairbourne
DISABLED:
Call in advance

Fairbourne village owes its existence to this line, which was laid in 1895 in order to transport building materials for the village's construction. It now runs from Fairbourne to Penrhyn Point, although there is an intermediate (but thankfully not a request) stop at Gorsafawddachaidraigodanhedogleddollonpenrhynareurdraethceredigion—the longest station name in the world. It's even longer in English, translating as 'The Mawddach station with its dragon's teeth on the northerly Penrhyn drive on the golden beach of Cardigan Bay'. Alight here for the nine-hole golf course. At Penrhyn Point the train connects with the ferry across the beautiful Afon Mawddach estuary to Barmouth.

HOW TO FIND US:
By car: Porthmadog is on the A487
Car parking: Onsite
By rail: Minfford and Blaenau Ffestiniog
ADDRESS: Harbour Station, Porthmadog, Gwynedd LL49 9NF
TEL: 01766 512 340
WEBSITE:
www.festrail.co.uk
LENGTH OF LINE:
13.5 miles
OPENING TIMES:
Daily from March to Nov, limited winter service
FACILITIES: Souvenir shop, licensed restaurant at Porthmadog
DISABLED: Wheelchair access at Porthmadog and Blaenau Ffestiniog, wheelchair facilities on trains by prior arrangement

FFESTINIOG

Past mountain lakes and waterfalls, through wide river valleys and thick oak forests, the trains of the Ffestiniog Railway chug their way through the natural glories of Snowdonia National Park. At its highest point, some 640ft above sea level, the views are quite simply breathtaking, stretching for miles on either side. Built in 1832 to carry slate from the mountain mines of Blaenau Ffestiniog to the port of Porthmadog, this is the oldest passenger-carrying narrow gauge railway in the world. Nearby attractions include the Llechwedd State Caverns and the architectural intensity of Portmeirion.

HOW TO FIND US:
By car: Llandudno is
on the A546
Car parking: 100 yds
from Lower Terminal
or adjacent to
Summit Terminal
By rail: Llandudno
ADDRESS: Victoria
Station, Church
Walks, Llandudno
TEL: 01492 574 229
LENGTH OF LINE:
Nearly 1 mile
OPENING TIMES:
Daily Easter–Oct
FACILITIES: Shops,
café, bar at Summit
Complex
DISABLED: Call in
advance

The Victorians came to Llandudno, the 'Queen of the Western Watering Places', in their thousands to take the waters and travel on its jolly little tramway. The tramline, Britain's only street funicular, climbs through the charming old town to the Country Park, home to many varieties of rare flora and fauna, as well as Great Orme's famous 4,000-year-old copper mines. At the summit, on a clear day, you can see as far as the Blackpool Tower and the Isle of Man.

LLANBERIS

HOW TO FIND US:
By car: Off the
A4086 Caernarfon to
Capel Curig road
Car parking: Onsite
By rail: Bangor
By bus: From
Bangor station to
Caernarfon. From
there, change for
Llanberis
ADDRESS:
Llanberis,
Caernafon LL55 4TY
TEL: 01286 870 549
LENGTH OF LINE:
2 miles
OPENING TIMES:
Mon–Fri & Sun
from May–Sep;
Sat July–Aug
FACILITIES:
Refreshments and
picnic area
Disabled: Wheel-
chair access to
shop and café at
Llanberis

See the snow-capped splendour of Snowdon aboard this gorgeous lakeside line. The trains run along the trackbed of a former slate railway through the Alt Wen woods, home to squirrels, woodpeckers and snakes, over the solidified lava of Volcano Cutting before finishing up at Cei Llydan, a great picnic spot with wonderful views of Mount Snowdon. At Llanberis you can visit the Dinorwic Quarry Workshops, now part of the National Museum of Wales.

HOW TO FIND US:
By car: Junction of the A5 and the A539
Car parking: Market Street in the town.
By rail: Ruabon
By bus:
Call 01978 860 701
ADDRESS: Abbey Road, Llangollen, Denbighshire, LL20 8SN
TEL: 01978 860 979
LENGTH OF LINE: 7.5 miles
OPENING TIMES: Most w/ends in the year; daily May–Oct
FACILITIES: Souvenir shop and tea shop,
DISABLED: Specially adapted carriage

The railway, the only preserved standard gauge line in North Wales, wends its way alongside the River Dee from Llangollen past the famous Horseshoe Falls, through the 689-yard Berwyn Tunnel to Carrog with its beautifully restored 1950s terminus. It is the railway's intention to extend the route a further 2.5 miles to Corwen in the near future. Driver experience courses are offered on both diesel and steam locomotives.

HOW TO FIND US:
By car: Llanberis Station is on the A4086,
Car parking: Pay and display at Llanberis
By rail: Bangor
By bus: From Bangor station to Caernarfon. From there, change for Llanberis
ADDRESS: Snowdon Mountain Railway, Llanberis LL55 4TY
TEL: 01286 870 223
LENGTH OF LINE: 5 miles
OPENING TIMES: Daily mid-Mar–early Nov
FACILITIES: Cafés at Llanberis and Summit
DISABLED: Wheelchair users are welcome. Please phone ahead

SNOWDON MOUNTAIN RAILWAY

This is one of the world's great railway journeys. Following the route of an old pony track, Swiss mountain steam and diesel engines haul passengers up through the cloud layer to the snow-capped peak of Mount Snowdon, 3,560ft above sea level. On a clear day, you can see not only the glorious splendour of Snowdonia National Park but the Isle of Man and, on occasions, even the green-tinged Wicklow Mountains across the Irish Sea. Should you feel the need to share your elevated experiences with the folks back home, write a quick postcard and pop it in the highest post box in the UK.

62

HOW TO FIND US:
By car: Tywyn is on the B4405
Car parking: On site
By rail: Tywyn
ADDRESS: Talyllyn Railway, Wharf Station, Tywyn, Gwynedd LL36 9EY
TEL: 01654 710 472
WEBSITE: www.talyllyn.co.uk
LENGTH OF LINE: 7.25 miles
OPENING TIMES: Sun late Feb–Mar; every day April–Oct; Specials in Dec
FACILITIES: Refreshments and souvenirs at Tywyn Wharf
DISABLED: Wheelchair access

Due to close in 1950 after 85 years of service, the Talyllyn Railway was saved by the world's first Railway Preservation Society. Not only did these enthusiasts ensure the continued survival of one of Wales' best loved railways but they provided inspiration and impetus for literally hundreds of other rail societies over the succeeding decades. The rich industrial heritage that Britain enjoys today is due in no small part to the efforts of the Talyllyn pioneers. The railway itself, still one of the most picturesque lines in the country, climbs through the thick wooded hills of the Snowdonia National Park from Tywyn Wharf to Nant Gwernol. All the passenger trains are hauled by steam engines and there is a small narrow gauge railway museum.

TEIFI VALLEY

HOW TO FIND US:
By car: Henllan is on the A484
Car parking: On site
By rail/bus: Carmarthen Station, from where the no. 461 bus runs to Henllan
ADDRESS: Henllan Station, Henllan, nr Newcastle Emlyn, Dyfed SA44 5TD
TEL: 01559 371 077
LENGTH OF LINE: 2 miles
OPENING TIMES: Mon–Thur April–Oct; Sun June –Sept
FACILITIES: Café, gift and souvenir shop, Railway Charity shop, baby changing facilities, picnic area
DISABLED: Wheelchair access

Situated near the famous market town of Newcastle Emlyn and operating on one of the few remaining sections of the Great Western Railway, the Teifi Valley Railway offers impressive views of the tree-clad Valley as it travels alongside the banks of the Teifi river and through large expanses of unspoilt woodland. At Henllan station, the starting point for various nature trails and country walks, there is a GWR pictoral museum and a new 'Dragon' miniature railway which takes a leisurely tour around the station gardens and locomotive sheds.

VALE OF GLAMORGAN

HOW TO FIND US:
By car: Barry is on the A4226, just off the A48
Car parking: On site
By rail: Services from Cardiff to Barry Island
ADDRESS: Barry Island Station, Barry Island, Vale of Glamorgan CF62 5TH
TEL: 01446 748 816
OPENING TIMES: Call in advance
FACILITIES: Refreshments, souvenir shop
DISABLED: Call in advance

The Vale of Glamorgan Railway Company was founded in 1994 to commemorate the enormous contribution made by steam railways to the development of South Wales in the 20th century and, in particular, to open a railway heritage centre at Barry Island. Few other towns have had such close links with the railway industry over the course of their history as Barry. In fact, Barry was brought into existence by the railways; founded by the Barry Dock and Railway Company in the 1880s as a coal-exporting port. The former station, platform and 11 engines have been restored and there are plans to operate a passenger-carrying service along a short length of track in the near future.

VALE OF RHEIDOL

HOW TO FIND US:
By car: Aberystwyth is on the A4120
Car parking: Available at Aberystwyth and Devil's Bridge
By rail: Aberystwyth
ADDRESS: Park Avenue, Aberystwyth, Cerdigion SY23 1PG
TEL: 01970 625 819
LENGTH OF LINE: 11.75 miles
OPENING TIMES: Trains run between Easter and Oct
FACILITIES: Refreshments and souvenir shop
DISABLED: Call in advance

In 1988, the Vale of Rheidol was the last steam railway still operated by British Rail. Unable to commit the funds necessary for its upkeep, the company sold it into private hands the very next year, since when it has been thoroughly restored and is now one of Wales' most popular railways. The journey runs for just under 12 miles, from Aberystwyth across the River Rheidol floodplain and up a steep climb to Devil's Bridge, 625ft above sea level. Here you can alight for a walk to the famous Devil's Bridge itself—in fact three bridges built one on top of the other, the first constructed, depending on who you believe, either by monks in the 11th century or by the Lord of the Flies himself—and the spectacular Devil's Falls.

WELSH HIGHLAND RAILWAY

HOW TO FIND US:
By car: On the A487
Tremadog Road
Car Parking: On site
By Rail: Porthmadog
ADDRESS:
Welsh Highland
Railway, Tremadog
Road, Porthmadog
LL49 9HP
TEL: 01766 513 402
24HR INFOLINE:
01766 513 402
WEBSITE: www.whr.
co.uk/WHR/
LENGTH OF LINE:
0.75 miles
OPENING TIMES:
W/ends from early
April–Oct
FACILITIES:
Café, souvenir and
book shop
DISABLED: Adapted
toilets

Here, a group of enthusiasts have joined together to rebuild and restore part of the Welsh Highland Railway which ran from 1922 until 1937. Today, you can take a short trip from Porthmadog to Gelert's Farm Works, where you can enjoy a free guided tour, and then on to the replica WHR halt at Pen-y-Mount. The carriages are pulled by a variety of locomotives; some travel behind 'Russell', the original company's sole surviving steam locomotive, while others are hauled by a LYd2 Romanian diesel engine—the most powerful of its type in Britain. There is also an opportunity to ride aboard the 'Gladstone' carriage, named after the great Victorian Prime Minister who once travelled on it during a holiday in Wales.

WELSHPOOL & LLANFAIR

HOW TO FIND US:
By car: Shrewsbury
Dongellau road A458
Car parking: On site
By rail: Welshpool
By bus: Midland Red
Buses to Welshpool
and Llanfair
ADDRESS: Llanfair
Caereinion, Powys
SY21 0SF
TEL: 01938 810 441
LENGTH OF LINE:
8 miles
OPENING TIMES:
W/ends and bank
holidays April–Sept;
daily mid-July–early
Sept and Oct half
term
FACILITIES: Tea
Room, book and
video shop, both at
Llanfair
DISABLED: Wheel-
chair access to both
trains and platforms,
2 adapted carriages,
adapted toilets

Locomotives from three continents travel along this eight-mile line, puffing their way through the pretty countryside, past farms and rivers and over startlingly steep hills, giving fantastic views of Welshpool's picturesque scenery. You can take the opportunity to negotiate the hills and bends for yourself on one of the Railway's Driving Experience courses, under the patient guidance of an experienced instructor. Canal boat trips are run at Welshpool, and the famous Powys Castle and Gardens are minutes away from the station.